Cracking the USACO Silver

A Comprehensive Guide to Succeeding in Competitive Programming

Eric Wang

Abstract

Cracking the USACO Silver is the ultimate resource for students preparing for the USACO competition. This book covers everything you need to know to succeed in the silver tier, including key problem-solving strategies, essential coding techniques, and advanced algorithms. With clear explanations and practical examples, this guidebook is perfect for anyone looking to improve their coding skills and achieve success in the competitive programming world. Whether you're a beginner or an experienced programmer, "Cracking the USACO Silver" is the perfect tool to help you take your coding skills to the next level.

Table of Contents

Preface

Code with Confidence: A Middle Schooler's Guide for Middle Schoolers!

Greetings, Code Warriors!

If you're reading this, you're about to embark on an epic quest to conquer the realm of USACO competitions. Fear not, for this trusty tome is your ultimate guide to achieving coding glory, filled with geeky wisdom, professional insights, and a healthy dose of humor that even the most stoic programmers can't resist.

In this action-packed adventure, you'll journey through the magical world of C++ programming, unlock the secrets of powerful data structures, and unleash the full potential of algorithms to vanquish your coding foes. Be prepared to face challenges worthy of a true Code Warrior, but worry not—our carefully crafted examples, illustrations, and exercises shall illuminate your path to victory.

From the humble beginnings of "Hello, World!" to the mind-bending complexities of recursion, you'll forge your coding skills in the fires of knowledge, tempering them with practice, and ultimately emerging as a master coder ready to take on the USACO competitions.

Along the way, you'll discover that we take our humor as seriously as our coding. After all, who said learning couldn't be fun? As you traverse the realms of control flow, data structures, and algorithmic techniques, you'll find quirky anecdotes and nerdy jokes to keep you entertained and motivated.

So, strap on your keyboard, adjust your ergonomic chair, and prepare to dive into the captivating world of competitive programming. Remember, the true measure of a Code Warrior lies not in the battles won but in the knowledge gained, the skills honed, and the friendships forged in the pursuit of coding excellence.

May the source (code) be with you!

Eric

Introduction

Ahoy there, fellow coding enthusiasts! Are you ready to venture into the exhilarating realm of programming, where every keystroke unlocks a universe of possibilities? Brace yourselves, for we are about to embark on an extraordinary journey into the world of competitive programming and USACO—a realm where challenges abound, algorithms reign supreme, and only the most valiant coders emerge victorious!

In this awe-inspiring section, we shall unravel the mysteries of programming, from the cryptic languages that power our digital domain to the mind-boggling problems that only the sharpest minds can solve. You'll learn the art of thinking like a programmer, uncovering the secrets of logic and reasoning that will propel you to the pinnacle of the coding pantheon.

As we delve into the fascinating world of competitive programming, we'll explore the ins and outs of USACO, the ultimate battleground for aspiring coding champions. You'll get a glimpse of the competition's structure, learn how to train for the battles ahead, and even pick up some nifty tips and tricks to outwit your fellow competitors.

Throughout this section, you'll encounter a delightful mix of geeky references, professional insights, and a generous sprinkling of humor to keep your spirits high and your brain cells buzzing. After all, who said learning can't be a rollercoaster ride of fun, excitement, and unbridled passion for programming?

So, put on your thinking caps, grab your favorite caffeinated beverage, and join us as we dive headfirst into the thrilling world of programming, competitive coding, and USACO. The adventure awaits, and the rewards are boundless for those who dare to dream, learn, and code!

Let the games begin!

Understanding USACO: Competitions, Structure and Practice

Competitive Coding - The Thrilling Arena of Algorithmic Gladiators

Welcome, brave souls, to the fantastic world of competitive coding! Here, intellects clash, problem-solvers collide, and the valiant warriors of the algorithmic realm vie for glory in a contest of wits and speed. But what is competitive coding, you ask? Why is it beneficial, and what can one expect from such a mind-bending pursuit? Fear not, for we shall unravel these enigmas together, armed with a fine blend of geekiness, professionalism, and a dash of humor to spice up the quest for knowledge.

Competitive coding, in a nutshell, is the intellectual equivalent of a high-octane, adrenaline-pumping sports showdown, where programmers flex their cerebral muscles to solve complex computational problems within a stipulated time frame. These battles of the brain often take place in online platforms, where contenders from across the globe engage in fierce algorithmic combat, seeking to outmaneuver one another in the quest for fame, fortune, and fabulous learning opportunities.

But why, you might wonder, should one partake in this arduous pastime? What can be gained from pitting one's wits against the clock and the collective intellect of fellow coders? The answer, my dear friends, is manifold:

1. Skill Enhancement: Hone your programming prowess, sharpen your problem-solving abilities, and master the art of algorithmic thinking, all while basking in the glorious challenge of competition.
2. Bragging Rights: Who wouldn't want to revel in the pride of being a coding champion, regaling friends and family with tales of algorithmic conquests and late-night debugging heroics?
3. Networking: Rub virtual elbows with fellow coding aficionados, forge lasting connections, and perhaps even collaborate on projects that could change the digital landscape.
4. Career Opportunities: Competitive coding is a magnet for recruiters, drawn to the allure of battle-tested programmers with a penchant for tackling the most intricate of problems.

As for expectations, competitive coding is a realm where anything can happen. One moment you might be devising an algorithm to herd virtual sheep across a field, the next, you could be calculating the optimal trajectory for an intergalactic pizza delivery service. The possibilities are as boundless as your imagination, and the rewards are well worth the effort.

So, ready your keyboards, don your coding armor, and prepare to embark on a journey of discovery, challenge, and exhilarating triumph. Competitive coding awaits, and with it, a chance to prove your mettle, expand your horizons, and join the ranks of the elite programmers who have conquered the algorithmic arena.

Global Coding Showdowns - Where the Young and the Geeky Conquer the World

Greetings, young coding prodigies, as we embark on a whirlwind tour of coding challenges that span the globe! From the frosty climes of the Arctic to the sweltering deserts of the Sahara, there's no corner of the world where the competitive coding spirit doesn't thrive. So, buckle up, and let's explore the multitude of programming tournaments where the brightest minds of high school and middle school compete for the ultimate prize - a lifetime of geeky glory.

1. The USACO (USA Computing Olympiad): Ah, the fabled land of the free and the home of the brave, where stars, stripes, and algorithms collide in the ultimate test of computational prowess. The USACO is a prestigious competition that offers four levels of difficulty - Bronze, Silver, Gold, and Platinum - designed to challenge and inspire even the most seasoned programming veterans.

2. The IOI (International Olympiad in Informatics): A global spectacle of algorithmic

grandeur, the IOI is the coding equivalent of the Olympics, where young geniuses from around the world gather to flex their programming muscles and compete for the coveted gold, silver, and bronze medals. With its nail-biting contests and heart-stopping showdowns, the IOI is a spectacle like no other.

3. The CCC (Canadian Computing Competition): Oh, Canada! The land of maple syrup, ice hockey, and coding contests that bring together the brightest young minds from coast to coast. The CCC is divided into Junior and Senior levels, catering to both middle school and high school students, who compete in a thrilling, problem-solving extravaganza that spans the vast and diverse Canadian landscape.

4. The Codeforces: A veritable mecca for competitive programmers, Codeforces is an online platform that hosts frequent contests, attracting a global community of coding enthusiasts who engage in brain-bending battles of skill and speed. With its ever-growing repository of problems and its vibrant community, Codeforces is a must-visit destination for any aspiring competitive coder.

5. The Google Code-in: Who wouldn't want a shot at impressing the world's most renowned tech giant? The Google Code-in is an annual competition aimed at pre-university students,

inviting them to contribute to open-source projects, solve real-world problems, and, of course, earn some serious bragging rights. Plus, the prospect of catching Google's attention is enough to make any coder's heart race with excitement.

6.   The Project Euler: For those who prefer a more solitary, contemplative coding experience, Project Euler offers a collection of challenging mathematical problems that require creative problem-solving and programming skills. It's an excellent training ground for sharpening one's computational abilities while indulging in some geeky introspection.

So there you have it, young coding warriors, a veritable smorgasbord of global coding challenges that await your talent and passion. Whether you're a high school hotshot or a middle school maven, there's a coding contest out there with your name on it. So, gather your wits, prepare your algorithms, and set forth on an international adventure that will test your skills, expand your horizons, and fill your life with geeky memories to last a lifetime.

USACO - The Ultimate Showdown of Algorithmic Titans

It's time to delve deep into the hallowed halls of the USA Computing Olympiad, a.k.a. USACO, the holy grail of competitive coding for American high school and middle school students. Prepare to embark on a thrilling journey through the mystical land of coding challenges, where fortunes are made, legends are born, and the geek shall inherit the earth!

The USACO is a prestigious, nationwide contest that provides young coders with the perfect platform to showcase their programming prowess and hone their skills in the fine art of algorithmic warfare. Founded in 1992, the USACO has, over the years, morphed into a multi-tiered battleground that spans four glorious levels of difficulty - Bronze, Silver, Gold, and Platinum - each designed to push you to your computational limits, and beyond.

But fear not, young warrior, for the USACO is not just about cutthroat competition and mind-bending puzzles. It's also an educational journey of epic proportions, filled with training pages, practice problems, and a wealth of resources that will help you sharpen your coding skills and ascend to the pantheon of programming legends.

Here's a step-by-step guide on how you can make the most of the USACO website to practice challenge coding and improve your problem-solving skills.

To begin, you need to register for a USACO account. Visit the USACO website at http://www.usaco.org/ and navigate to the registration page. Fill in the required details, including your name, email address, and a unique username. After completing the registration form, you will receive an email containing your password, which you can use to log into your account.

Once you have successfully logged in, start exploring the various contest problems available on the site. You can access them by clicking on the "Training" or "Contests" tabs on the top navigation bar. The problems are organized by difficulty level and contest date, allowing you to choose the most suitable challenges based on your skill level and interests. Each problem comes with a detailed problem statement, input/output specifications, and sample test cases to help you understand the requirements.

When you have selected a problem, read the problem statement carefully and start working on a solution using your preferred programming language. It's essential to write clean, efficient, and well-organized code, as USACO problems often test your ability to solve complex problems under strict time and memory constraints.

After you have written and tested your code locally, it's time to submit your solution on the USACO website. Navigate to the problem page and scroll down to the submission section. Choose the appropriate programming language from the dropdown menu and upload your source code file. Alternatively, you can copy and paste your code into the provided text box. Make sure to follow any specific naming or formatting requirements mentioned in the problem statement.

Finally, click on the "Submit" button and wait for the automated judging system to evaluate your solution. The evaluation process may take a few minutes, depending on the complexity of the problem and the number of submissions in the queue. Once your submission is judged, you will receive a detailed report with your score, as well as a breakdown of your performance on each test case. This feedback can help you identify any weaknesses in your code or logic and make improvements for future challenges.

By following these steps and consistently practicing on the USACO website, you can sharpen your problem-solving and programming skills and preparing yourself for success in competitive programming contests.

C++ Conquest: A Geek's Guide to Mastering the Magic of Programming

Welcome, intrepid code crusaders, to the enchanted realm of C++ programming! In this thrilling section, we shall embark on a grand adventure, delving into the arcane arts of variables, loops, and logic operations that form the very foundation of this powerful language. With a sprinkling of geeky charm, a dash of professional expertise, and a hearty helping of humor, we'll transform you into a bona fide C++ wizard, ready to cast your spell on the competitive coding world.

As any seasoned sorcerer knows, a strong foundation is key to mastering the mystical forces of programming. Fear not, for in this sacred tome, we shall reveal the secrets of the C++ lexicon, guiding you through the labyrinth of syntax and semantics that make this language a favorite among coding champions the world over.

So, buckle up, my eager apprentices, as we journey through the hallowed halls of C++ programming. We'll conjure up variables and wield mathematical operations with the finesse of a true coding maestro. We'll summon the powers of control flow, bending the very fabric of code to our will with if-else statements. And, of course, we'll master the mystical art of looping, harnessing the boundless energy of for and while loops to achieve the impossible.

Prepare yourself for a wild ride through the bewitching world of C++ programming, where geeks reign supreme, professionalism is paramount, and humor is the secret ingredient that makes it all so much fun. With our trusty guide by your side, you'll soon find yourself wielding the full might of the C++ language, ready to take on the fiercest coding challenges the USACO can throw your way.

So, grab your magic wand (or keyboard, as the case may be), and let the adventure begin!

Say Hello to C++: Your First 'Hello, World!' Program

Welcome to the world of C++ programming. In this chapter, we will dive into the magical realm of your very first C++ program: the legendary 'Hello, World!'. It might not be as thrilling as casting spells at Hogwarts, but hey, who wouldn't want to make a computer talk?

First things first, let's take a look at our mighty 'Hello, World!' program:

Now, don't panic! We will break down this code snippet piece by piece like a LEGO set, and you'll be a C++ wizard in no time.

1. `#include <iostream></pre>`: This line is like a VIP pass that grants us access to the I/O (input/output) stream library. It's the secret

sauce that enables us to use std::cout and std::endl in our program.

2. int main()
    : Behold the main function, the heart and soul of our program! It's where the execution begins and ends. The int part signals that our main function will return an integer value when it's done doing its thing.

3. {}
    : These curly braces are like the loving arms of a code hug. They envelop everything inside the main function and keep our code organized.

4. std::cout << "Hello, World!" << std::endl;
    : Now, this line is where the magic happens. std::cout is our trusty tool for printing text to the console, and it's like a conveyor belt carrying our precious "Hello, World!" message to the screen. The << operator is the wizard's wand that directs the flow of data. Finally, std::endl is the polite way to say, "That's it for now, let's start a new line."

5. return 0;
    : This line is like the final bow at the end of a performance. It tells the program, "Bravo, you've done a fantastic job. Now, go ahead and return the integer value 0 to signal that everything went smoothly."

And there you have it! With the power of C++, you've successfully made your computer say "Hello, World!" Give yourself a pat on the back, and let's continue our journey into the enchanting universe of programming. Stay tuned for more thrilling (and geeky) adventures!

Setting Up Your C++ Battlestation: Mac & Windows Edition

Ahoy, future code warriors! Before you can embark on your grand programming adventures, you'll need to prepare your trusty steed (aka your computer) for battle. Whether you're a Mac aficionado or a Windows devotee, we've got you covered. Follow our trusty guide, and you'll be slaying code dragons in no time.

For Mac Users: Xcode to the Rescue

If you're on team Mac, Apple has graciously bestowed upon us the mighty Xcode, an all-in-one tool that's perfect for your C++ needs. Here's how to get it:

1. Open the Mac App Store (the blue icon with a giant "A" that's probably hiding in your dock).
2. Search for "Xcode" in the top-right corner and click "Get" to download this magical tool.
3. Once installed, open Xcode and follow the on-screen prompts to complete the setup.

Now, let's create your first C++ project in Xcode:

1. Launch Xcode and select "Create a new Xcode project."

2. Choose "macOS" and then "Command Line Tool" as your template.
3. Give your project a cool name (we suggest "CodeWarrior") and set "Language" to "C++".
4. Choose a location to save your project, and Xcode will create a shiny new C++ playground for you!

To run your program, just click the "Play" button (or press Cmd + R), and watch your code come to life!

For Windows Users: Visual Studio, Assemble!

Fear not, Windows users, we haven't forgotten about you! Microsoft's Visual Studio is your go-to weapon for C++ programming. Here's how to wield it:

1. Open your favorite browser and navigate to the Visual Studio download page: https://visualstudio.microsoft.com/downloads/
2. Download the "Community" edition, which is free and perfect for budding code warriors like you.
3. Run the installer and select the "Desktop development with C++" workload to get all the C++ goodness.
4. Follow the installation wizard's steps, and soon you'll have Visual Studio ready for action!

Now, let's create your first C++ project in Visual Studio:

1. Launch Visual Studio and select "Create a new project."
2. Choose "Console App" as your project type and click "Next."
3. Give your project an epic name (maybe "CodeCrusader"?) and click "Create" to start your journey.
4. Visual Studio will generate a new C++ project, complete with a "Hello, World!" program to kick things off.

To run your program, hit F5 or click the green "Local Windows Debugger" button, and watch your masterpiece unfold!

Congratulations, dear code warriors! You've successfully set up your C++ programming environment on either Mac or Windows. Now, the real adventure begins. Strap on your coding helmet, grab your keyboard, and charge into the fray! The world of C++ awaits!

Running C++ Online: A Magical Portal to the Coding Realm

Greetings, fellow code wizards! Are you itching to dive into the enchanting world of C++ but feel shackled by the limitations of your trusty computer? Fear not, for we have just the incantation to grant you passage into the ethereal plane of online coding! Read on, and we shall reveal the mystical secrets of running C++ code in the boundless realms of cyberspace.

The Online Compiler Kingdom: cpp.sh

In the land of online compilers, cpp.sh reigns supreme as a powerful, easy-to-use, and reliable portal to the world of C++ programming. With just a few simple steps, you'll be casting powerful code spells in no time:

1. Open your trusty browser and navigate to the mystical realm of http://cpp.sh/.
2. Behold the shimmering coding canvas that awaits you! Here, you can write, edit, and run your very own C++ programs.
3. Click the "Run" button (or press Ctrl + Enter) to unleash the raw power of your code.
4. Observe the "Output" window to witness the awe-inspiring fruits of your labor.

The Magical Compiler Forest: Replit

Another enchanted destination in the realm of online compilers is Replit (https://replit.com/), a versatile and user-friendly platform for code conjurers like you:

1. Summon your browser and set forth on your journey to https://replit.com/.
2. Click "Start coding" to begin your adventure, and select "C++" as your language of choice.

3. You'll be transported to a magical realm where you can craft, edit, and execute your C++ programs.
4. Click the "Run" button (or press Ctrl + Enter) to bring your code to life and observe the results in the console.

The Compiler Elders: Compiler Explorer and OnlineGDB

For the more seasoned code sorcerers among you, the Compiler Explorer (https://godbolt.org/) and OnlineGDB (https://www.onlinegdb.com/) offer deeper insight into the arcane arts of C++ compilation:

1. Visit either https://godbolt.org/ or https://www.onlinegdb.com/ and select "C++" as your language.
2. Craft your spell (aka write your C++ program) in the provided editor.
3. Invoke the "Run" or "Compile & Execute" button to unleash your code's hidden potential.
4. Examine the output and, if you dare, explore the generated assembly code to glimpse the inner workings of your C++ incantations.

And there you have it, noble code wizards! With these enchanted online portals at your disposal, you can now wield the mighty power of C++ from anywhere in the realm. No longer shall your coding prowess be limited by the confines of your trusty steed (aka your computer). Venture forth and conquer the mystical world of C++ programming!

1.   What is the purpose of the main() function in a C++ program?

Answer: The main() function is the entry point of a C++ program. When the program is executed, the main() function is called first, and the code inside the function is executed sequentially.

The Magical World of Variables, Types, and Comments in C++ – Example Code

Welcome, brave code wizard! In this enchanting chapter, we'll venture into the mystical realm of C++ variables, primitive data types, assignment, and comments. Let's conjure up a spellbinding program to unveil the arcane secrets behind these concepts.

In this mystical program, we first create two integer variables,

magicalNumber

and

enchantingMultiplier

. These integers store whole numbers, like the number of spells in your grimoire or the quantity of potions in your satchel.

Next, we call forth a double variable,

mysticFraction

, which can store decimal values. Double variables are perfect for calculating the potency of your potions or the efficiency of your elixirs.

Now, the arcane art of calculation begins! We multiply

magicalNumber

by

enchantingMultiplier

and store the result in

spellboundResult

. This demonstrates the power of the assignment operator = and how it can store the results of our mystical math.

We then weave the magic of our double variable,

mysticFraction

, into our calculations. By multiplying

spellboundResult

by

mysticFraction

, we concoct a potion of incredible strength, stored in the

potionStrength

variable.

Finally, we reveal our sorcerous secrets to the world with the mystical

std::cout

command. This enchanted command allows us to display our wondrous results on the screen for all to see.

Throughout the program, you'll notice the magical incantations, known as comments, which begin with

//

. These enchanted words are for us code wizards to communicate and share our arcane knowledge while leaving the compiler undisturbed.

And so, the mystery of C++ variables, primitive data types, assignment, and comments has been unveiled! With this newfound power, you are one step closer to becoming a true code sorcerer.

C++ Variables Unleashed: Naming, Changing, and Taming the Constants

Welcome, code adventurer! In this thrilling chapter, we'll embark on a quest to explore the world of C++ variables, learn the secret art of naming, discover how to change their values, and unveil the mysteries of declaring constants. Arm yourself with knowledge as we introduce the concepts of variables, primitive data types, assignment, and comments in the legendary C++ realm!

In this mind-blowing program, we set out on our adventure by creating a variable of type

int

named

lightYears

. In the universe of C++, variables need to have a name and a type. The type determines the kind of values a variable can store, while the name lets us identify and manipulate the variable.

When choosing a name for our variables, it's crucial to follow good naming practices. A variable's name should be descriptive and embrace the "camelCase" convention, where each word starts with a capital letter except for the first one, as demonstrated in

numberOfPlanets

and

planetMass

.

The secret power of a true coder lies in their ability to change a variable's value. In our program, we showcase this remarkable skill by adding 10 to

lightYears

. The assignment operator

=

enables us to store the new value in the variable.

Sometimes, code warriors must create unbreakable constants, which are declared using the

const

keyword, followed by the type and the variable name. In our program, we declare a constant

speedOfLight

that remains immutable.

At last, we reveal the results of our extraordinary journey using the mighty

std::cout

command. This powerful tool allows us to display our awe-inspiring discoveries on the screen for the world to see.

As you continue your journey through the C++ cosmos, remember the invaluable knowledge you've gained about variables, naming conventions, value manipulation, and constants. This wisdom will guide you in your quest to become a legendary code master.

C++ Constants

In C++, constants are values that cannot be modified during the execution of a program. They play a crucial role in making the code more robust, maintainable, and easier to understand. In this section, we will discuss different ways to define constants in C++ and some best practices for using them.

There are several ways to define constants in C++:

1. Using const keyword: You can use the const keyword to create a constant variable. Once initialized, its value cannot be changed.

2. Using constexpr keyword: This is a C++11 feature, allowing you to define a constant expression that is evaluated at compile-time. It ensures that the constant value is determined before the program runs.

3. Using #define directive: The #define preprocessor directive is another way to define constants. It replaces all occurrences of

the constant with its value during the preprocessing phase before compilation.

4. Using enumeration: Enumerations are user-defined data types that consist of a set of named integer constants. They are ideal for representing a group of related constant values.

Best Practices for Using Constants

1. Naming conventions: It's a good practice to use uppercase letters and underscores to name constants, making it easier to distinguish them from regular variables.

2. Use const or constexpr over #define: Using const or constexpr is generally preferred over #define, as they provide better type safety and follow the C++ scoping rules.

3. Use constants for magic numbers: Replace any hardcoded values (magic numbers) in your code with named constants, making your code more readable and maintainable.

4. Use constexpr for compile-time calculations: If you have a constant expression that can be computed at compile-time, use constexpr. This can help optimize your code by performing calculations before the program runs.

5. Group related constants using enumerations: When you have a set of related constant values, use enumerations to group them logically, making the code more organized and easier to understand.

Constants are an essential part of C++ programming, helping you write more reliable and maintainable code. By understanding how to define constants and following best practices, you can improve the overall quality of your programs.

1. Question: What are the rules for naming variables in C++?

Answer: The rules for naming variables in C++ are:

```
Variable names must start with a letter or an
underscore (_).
They can contain letters, digits, and undersc
ores.
Variable names are case-sensitive.
They must not be C++ reserved keywords.
```

Explanation: Following these rules ensures that variable names are unique, easily recognizable, and do not conflict with reserved keywords.

2. Question: How do you declare a variable in C++?

Answer: To declare a variable in C++, you need to specify the data type followed by the variable name. Optionally, you can also assign an initial value.

Example:

Explanation: In the example, we declare an integer variable named my_number and a float variable named my_float initialized with the value 3.14. The variable names must follow the naming conventions and should not conflict with reserved keywords.

3. Question: What is the purpose of the const keyword?

Answer: The const keyword is used to declare a constant variable, which cannot be modified after its initialization.

Example:

Explanation: In the example, we declare a constant integer variable named days_in_week and initialize it with the value 7. Once initialized, the value of this variable cannot be changed during the program execution, ensuring that the value remains constant throughout the program.

4. Question: What is the difference between assignment and initialization in C++?

Answer: Initialization sets a variable's value when it is declared, while assignment assigns a new value to an existing variable.

Example:

Explanation: In the example, the variable a is initialized with the value 5 when it is declared. Later, its value is updated through assignment with the new value 10.

5. Question: Can you assign a value of one data type to a variable of another data type in C++? Explain with an example.

Answer: Yes, you can assign a value of one data type to a variable of another data type, but it may result in data loss or truncation if the target data type cannot represent the full range or precision of the source data type.

Example:

Explanation: In this example, an integer value 3 is assigned to a float variable my_float. The assignment is allowed, and the value of my_float will be 3.0. However, if the source data type has a larger range or higher precision than the target data type, the value might be truncated or lose precision during the assignment.

6. Question: What is the syntax for declaring multiple variables of the same data type in a single line?

Answer: To declare multiple variables of the same data type in a single line, use a comma-separated list of variable names after the data type.

Example:

Explanation: In the example, three integer variables x, y, and z are declared in a single line. This is a more concise way to declare multiple variables of the same data type.

7. Question: What happens if you use an uninitialized variable in C++?

Answer: Using an uninitialized variable in C++ can lead to undefined behavior, as the variable may contain a garbage value.

Explanation: When a variable is declared without initialization, its value is not set to a default value, and it contains whatever data was previously stored at that memory location. Using uninitialized variables can result in unpredictable behavior and hard-to-find bugs in your program. It is always a good practice to initialize variables before using them.

C++ Comments: The Art of Whispering to Your Code

Greetings, intrepid coder! In this enchanting chapter, we will embark on a magical journey into the secret world of C++ comments. These mystical incantations allow you to speak directly to your code, sharing wisdom and guidance for future generations of code sorcerers. But fear not! We shall delve into the arcane arts of using comments and unveil their hidden utility.

Behold, the two styles of C++ comments that hold the power to unveil the secrets of your code:

Single-line comments are denoted by two slashes

```
//
```

and shall vanish at the end of the line. The multi-line comments, however, are more mysterious. They are marked by a

```
/*
```

at the beginning and a

```
*/
```

at the end. Within these symbols, your words of wisdom shall be safely ensconced, spanning multiple lines.

But why, you may ask, do these mystical commentaries serve a purpose in the realm of C++? Fear not, for the answer is revealed:

1. Enlightening fellow code mages: Comments serve as a guiding light, illuminating the intentions of your code for others who dare to explore its depths.
2. Chronicling your own heroic journey: As time passes, even the most formidable code sorcerer may forget the purpose of their spells. Comments preserve your wisdom, so you may recall your intentions with ease.
3. Temporarily banishing sections of your code: Sometimes, a code mage must temporarily suppress the power of a spell, to test its strength or to debug its effects. By conjuring comments, you can swiftly disable sections of your code without destroying them.

In this enchanted program, we demonstrate the power of comments to guide our fellow mages and suppress spells. As you continue your quest to become a legendary code sorcerer, never forget the value of sharing wisdom and preserving the secrets of your code through the magical art of C++ comments.

Exercises: C++ Comments: The Art of Whispering to Your Code

1. Question: What are the two types of comments in C++?

Answer: The two types of comments in C++ are:

- Single-line comments: They start with
  `//`
  and continue to the end of the line.
- Multi-line comments: They start with
  `/*`
  and end with
  `*/`
  .

Explanation: Single-line comments are used for short explanations or to temporarily disable a line of code, while multi-line comments are used for longer explanations or to disable multiple lines of code at once.

2. Question: How do you write a single-line comment in C++?

Answer: To write a single-line comment in C++, start the comment with

`//`

followed by the comment text.

Example:

Explanation: In the example, the text following `//` is a single-line comment, and it does not affect the execution of the code.

3. Question: How do you write a multi-line comment in C++?

Answer: To write a multi-line comment in C++, start the comment with

```
/*
```

and end it with

```
*/
```

.

Example:

Explanation: In the example, the text between /* and */ is a multi-line comment, and it does not affect the execution of the code. Multi-line comments can span multiple lines of text.

4. Question: Can comments be nested in C++?

Answer: Single-line comments can be nested within multi-line comments, but multi-line comments cannot be nested within each other.

Example: ⟮

Explanation: In the example, the single-line comment is nested within the multi-line comment, which is allowed. However, attempting to nest a multi-line comment within another multi-line comment will result in a syntax error.

5. Question: What is the purpose of comments in C++ code?

Answer: The purpose of comments in C++ code is to:

- Explain the purpose and functionality of the code.
- Make the code more readable and understandable for others or for yourself when revisiting the code later.
- Temporarily disable a line or block of code during debugging or testing.

Explanation: Comments are not executed by the compiler and do not affect the functionality of the code. They serve as a means to document and explain the code to make it easier for others to understand or to remind yourself of how the code works when revisiting it later. Additionally, comments can be used to temporarily disable parts of the code during debugging or testing.

C++ Data Types: The Building Blocks of Code Alchemy

Greetings, code sorcerer apprentice! Prepare for an exhilarating journey into the realm of C++ data types, where we shall uncover the building blocks of your alchemical coding creations. These mystical elements bind together to form more complex spells and incantations, weaving the tapestry of your code.

Behold, the primary C++ data types that form the foundation of your arcane arts:

1. int
   : The humble integer, capable of holding whole numbers, both positive and negative. It is a stalwart companion in many a code mage's arsenal. Beware its limitations, for its maximum and minimum value may vary depending on your compiler and system.

2. float
   : The enigmatic float, a master of decimal numbers, stores values with a fractional part. Though it is a powerful ally, its precision is limited by its 32-bit storage capacity. Approach with caution, for it may lead to unforeseen inaccuracies.

3. double
   : The more precise sibling of the float, the double holds twice the power in its 64-bit storage. It maintains greater precision, but it also demands more memory as tribute.

4. char
   : The mysterious char, a keeper of individual characters. It stores a single character, encoded in the ancient tongue of ASCII. It is a versatile ally, capable of serving as both a number and a symbol.

5. bool
   : The enigmatic bool, a master of duality. It knows only two states: true and false. It is the

guardian of logic, casting the ultimate judgment upon your code's conditions.

In this captivating program, we conjure the power of each data type and reveal their secrets. As you traverse the treacherous landscapes of coding, remember that choosing the right data type is vital to the success of your code alchemy. May you wield these mystical building blocks with wisdom, as you ascend to the pinnacle of code sorcery.

1. Question: What are the four primary data types in C++?

Answer: The four primary data types in C++ are:

- int (integer)
- float (floating-point number)
- double (double-precision floating-point number)
- char (character)

Explanation: These data types are used to represent different kinds of data in a C++ program. Integers are whole numbers, floats and doubles are used for real numbers (doubles provide more precision than floats), and chars represent single characters.

2. Question: What is the difference between a float and a double in C++?

Answer: The main difference between a float and a double in C++ is the precision and range they can represent. Floats have single-precision, while doubles have double-precision, which means that doubles can represent a larger range and more accurate values than floats.

Explanation: Floats use 4 bytes of memory and typically have a precision of about 6-7 decimal digits, while doubles use 8 bytes of memory and have a precision of about 15-17 decimal digits. This increased precision allows doubles to represent larger numbers and more accurate decimal values than floats.

3. Question: How do you declare a variable with a specific data type in C++?

Answer: To declare a variable with a specific data type in C++, you need to specify the data type followed by the variable name. Optionally, you can also assign a value to the variable during declaration.

Example:

Explanation: In the example, four variables are declared with different data types: an int, a float, a double, and a char. Each variable is assigned an initial value during declaration.

4. Question: What is the purpose of the sizeof()
operator in C++?

Answer: The

sizeof()

operator in C++ is used to determine the size (in bytes) of a data type or a variable of a specific data type.

Example:

Explanation: In the example, the

sizeof()

operator is used to display the size of the int data type and the size of the

myInt

variable. Both values will be the same, as

myInt

is of type int.

5. Question: What is the difference between signed and unsigned integer types in C++?

Answer: The main difference between signed and unsigned integer types in C++ is that signed integers can represent both positive and negative values, while unsigned integers can only represent non-negative values.

Explanation: Signed integers use one bit to represent the sign of the number, while the remaining bits represent the magnitude. Unsigned integers use all bits to represent the magnitude, allowing for a larger range of positive values but not allowing for negative values. For example, an unsigned 8-bit integer can represent values from 0 to 255, while a signed 8-bit integer can represent values from -128 to 127.

6. Question: What are the basic data types in C++?

Answer: The basic data types in C++ are int, float, double, char, and bool.

Explanation: These data types represent different types of data, such as integers, floating-point numbers, characters, and boolean values (true or false). They are used to declare variables in C++ programs.

7. Question: What is the difference between int and float data types?

Answer: int is used for storing integer values, while float is used for storing floating-point numbers.

Explanation: Integer values are whole numbers without a decimal part, while floating-point numbers have both an integer part and a decimal part. The int data type uses less memory and is generally faster for arithmetic operations compared to float.

8. Question: What is the purpose of the bool data type?

Answer: The bool data type is used to represent boolean values, either true or false.

Explanation: Boolean values are used in conditional expressions and control structures, such as if statements and loops. They are the result of logical and comparison operations.

C++ Mathemagics: Conjuring Calculations and Casting Spells"

Greetings, aspiring code wizards! Prepare to embark on a thrilling adventure into the mystical realm of C++ math operations, where we shall unveil the secrets of casting spells, prioritizing incantations, and harnessing the power of self-assigning operations.

Behold, the elemental C++ math operations that shall empower you to conjure potent calculations:

1. **Addition** (+): Summon the forces of arithmetic to unite two numbers and create a more formidable value.
2. **Subtraction** (-): With precision, cleave a number asunder, separating the essence of its value.
3. **Multiplication** (*): Multiply your power and unleash the full potential of your numbers.
4. **Division** (/): Divide and conquer, partitioning your numeric foes into more manageable fragments.

5. **Modulus** (%): The arcane remainder operation, a divination tool for discerning the residue of a division.

As you delve deeper into the mathemagical arts, remember to master the following techniques:

1. **Casting**: Harness the power of transformation, bending data types to your will. Cast one type into another with the finesse of a true sorcerer, but beware the consequences of truncation or loss of precision.
2. **Priority**: Like a grand symphony, your incantations must be orchestrated in the proper sequence. Respect the natural order of operations, giving precedence to multiplication and division over addition and subtraction.
3. **Self-assigning Operations**: Unleash the power of shorthand and elegance with self-assigning operations (+=, -=, *=, /=, %=). Invoke the magic within your variables, updating their values in a single incantation.

As you wield these enchanting mathemagical tools, may you bring balance and harmony to the code realms, transcending the mundane and achieving the extraordinary.

1. Question: What are the basic arithmetic operators in C++?

Answer: The basic arithmetic operators in C++ are:

- Addition: +
- Subtraction: -
- Multiplication: *
- Division: /
- Modulus (remainder): %

Explanation: These operators allow you to perform basic arithmetic operations on numeric values in a C++ program. They can be used with integer, float, and double data types.

2. Question: What is the difference between integer division and floating-point division in C++?

Answer: In C++, integer division truncates any decimal portion of the result, while floating-point division retains the decimal portion.

Example:

Explanation: In the example, when dividing two integers, the decimal portion is truncated, resulting in an integer value. When dividing a float by an integer, floating-point division is performed, and the decimal portion is retained.

3.   Question: Read the following code and determine its output:

Answer: The output of the code will be 1.

Explanation: The code calculates the remainder of the division of a (10) by b (3) using the modulus operator (%). The remainder of 10 divided by 3 is 1, so the output will be 1.

4.   Question: Write a C++ code snippet that calculates the area of a circle with a radius of 5.0 and displays the result. (Assume PI = 3.14159)

Answer:

Explanation: In this example, we declare a

double

variable

radius

with a value of 5.0, and a

double

constant

PI

with a value of 3.14159. We then calculate the area using the formula

area = PI * radius * radius

and display the result.

5. Question: What is the result of the following expression in C++?

Answer: The result of the expression will be

12

.

Explanation: Following the order of operations, the expression is evaluated as follows:

Thus, the value of

x

is

12

.

C++ Boolean Brouhaha: Unraveling the Mysteries of True and False

Greetings, code conjurers! Prepare to enter the enigmatic realm of C++ Boolean operations, where truth and falsehood collide in a spectacular dance of logic. We shall delve into the mystic arts of Boolean alchemy, exploring priority and the curious incantations that govern the balance between true and false.

Behold, the elemental C++ Boolean operations that shall empower you to bend the fabric of truth:

1. AND (&&): A binding spell that requires the truth of both operands to unleash its full potential.
2. OR (||): An inclusive charm that calls forth truth if either operand holds its power.
3. NOT (!): A negation hex that inverts the essence of truth, transforming it into its antithesis.

As you embark on this mesmerizing journey, remember to acquaint yourself with the following mysteries:

1. **Priority**: In the grand tapestry of logic, weave your spells with precision and care. The natural order of operations must be respected, with NOT taking precedence over AND, and AND over OR.

2. **Parentheses**: Like a masterful artisan, shape your incantations with the elegance of parentheses, guiding the flow of truth through your code and ensuring the correct order of operations.

As you unravel the enigmatic secrets of C++ Boolean operations, may you find solace in the balance between truth and falsehood, weaving a spellbinding tale of code and logic that transcends the ordinary.

Exercises: C++ Boolean Brouhaha: Unraveling the Mysteries of True and False

1. Question: What are the basic boolean (logical) operators in C++?

Answer: The basic boolean operators in C++ are:

AND: &&
OR: ||
NOT: !

Explanation: These operators allow you to perform logical operations on boolean values in a C++ program. They can be used in conditional statements and loops to control the flow of the program based on the truthiness of certain conditions.

2. Question: What is the difference between the
&&
(AND) and
||
(OR) operators in C++?

Answer: The && (AND) operator returns true if both operands are

true

, and

false

otherwise. The

||

(OR) operator returns

true

if at least one of the operands is

true

, and

false

otherwise.

Explanation: These operators are used to combine multiple boolean expressions in a C++ program. The

&&

operator is used when all conditions must be met, while the

||

operator is used when at least one of the conditions must be met.

3. Question: Read the following code and determine its output:

Answer: The output of the code will be 0.

Explanation: The code calculates the result of the boolean expression

a && b

using the AND operator (&&). Since

a

is true and

b

is

false

, the expression evaluates to

false

. In C++, boolean values are displayed as integers:

true

is displayed as 1, and

false

is displayed as

0

. Thus, the output will be

0

.

    4.   Question: Write a C++ code snippet that checks if a given integer x is positive and even, and displays "Yes" if it is, or "No" otherwise.

Answer:

Explanation: In this example, we declare an int variable x with a value of 4. We then use a conditional statement with the AND operator (&&) to check if x is positive (x > 0) and even (x % 2 == 0). If both conditions are true, we display "Yes", otherwise, we display "No".

    5.   Question: What is the result of the following boolean expression in C++?

Answer: The result of the expression will be

true

.

Explanation: Following the order of operations, the expression is evaluated as follows:

Thus, the value of

x

is

true

.

C++ Control Flow Chronicles: Embarking on an If-Else Adventure

Greetings, code wizards! Ready your wands and summon your inner geek, for we're about to embark on a thrilling journey through the enchanted lands of C++ control flow. With the power of if, if..else, and if else if else, we shall weave a spellbinding tale of code that bends to our will.

First, let us invoke the mighty

if

statement, a solitary sentinel that stands guard over a block of code:

Fear not, for the cunning

if..else

statement shall heed your call, offering a second path should the condition falter:

Behold the almighty

if else if else

statement, a majestic cascade of conditions that shall carve a path through the complexities of code:

As we venture forth into the realm of C++ control flow, let us weave a tapestry of if, if..else, and if else if else statements that shall dazzle the mind and captivate the imagination:

Armed with the arcane knowledge of C++ control flow, you shall forge a path through the labyrinthine logic of code, conquering the challenges that lie in wait with the power of

if

,

if..else

, and

if else if else

.

Example: 2018 February Contest, Bronze Problem 1. Teleportation

Problem

Farmer John, a true innovator in the world of agriculture, has grown tired of the tedious task of hauling cow manure across his farm. In a stroke of genius, he invents the marvelous manure teleporter! Now he can instantly zap manure between two points, making the tractor and cart combo a thing of the past.

Farmer John's farm is a linear masterpiece, stretching out along a single straight road. This means that any location on the farm can be represented by a point on the number line. The teleporter is defined by two coordinates, x and y, where manure at location x can be teleported to location y (and vice versa).

Our innovative farmer wants to move manure from point a to point b, and he's built a teleporter that may or may not be useful in this process (of course, he's not obliged to use the teleporter if it doesn't help). Your mission, should you choose to accept it, is to help Farmer John calculate the minimum distance he needs to haul the manure with his trusty tractor. Let the manure teleportation commence!

Analyze

Greetings, fellow manure teleportation enthusiasts! Today, we find ourselves presented with a challenge that combines the best of farming and cutting-edge technology. To fully appreciate the nuances of this problem, let's break it down into digestible, manure-sized chunks.

1. The farm's layout: We know that Farmer John's farm is a beautiful, linear arrangement that stretches along a single straight road. This simplifies matters as we only need to consider one-dimensional distances.

2. Teleporter mechanics: The manure teleporter operates using two coordinates, x and y, allowing for instant teleportation between

these points. Importantly, the teleportation works both ways.

3. Manure transportation: Farmer John's objective is to transport manure from location a to location b. The teleporter may be helpful in this process, but it's not mandatory. We need to figure out if using the teleporter can minimize the hauling distance.

4. Calculating the minimum distance: Our goal is to help Farmer John determine the shortest distance he must haul the manure with his tractor. We'll need to consider different scenarios, comparing the distance with and without using the teleporter.

So, fellow problem solvers, grab your pitchforks and don your thinking caps! Together, we'll dive into the exhilarating world of manure teleportation and help Farmer John optimize his futuristic farming operations. Remember, when it comes to teleporting manure, the sky's the limit!

Solution

Exercises: C++ Control Flow Chronicles: Embarking on an If-Else Adventure

1. Question: What are the three basic conditional statements in C++?

Answer: The three basic conditional statements in C++ are:

```
if
if-else
if-else if-else
```

Explanation: Conditional statements are used to control the flow of a program based on specific conditions. The

if

statement checks if a single condition is

true

, the

if-else

statement checks if a condition is

true

and provides an alternative path if it is false, and the

if-else if-else

statement checks for multiple conditions and provides alternative paths for each condition.

2. Question: What is the purpose of the
   else
   statement in C++?

Answer: The

else

statement provides an alternative path of execution when the condition in the preceding

if

statement is false.

Explanation: The

else

statement is used after an

if

statement to specify the code block that should be executed when the condition in the

if

statement is not met (

false

). It allows for more complex decision-making in a program.

3. Question: Read the following code and determine its output:

Answer: The output of the code will be Odd.

Explanation: The code checks if the remainder of

x

divided by 2 is equal to 0 using the modulo operator (%). If the condition is true, it means x is even, and the program outputs "Even". Otherwise, it means

x

is odd, and the program outputs "Odd". Since 7 is an odd number, the output will be "Odd".

4. Question: Write a C++ code snippet that reads an integer from the user and checks if it is positive, negative, or zero, displaying the appropriate message for each case.

Answer:

Explanation: In this example, we declare an

int

variable

x

and read its value from the user using cin. We then use an

if-else if-else

statement to check if

x

is positive, negative, or zero, and display the appropriate message for each case.

5. Question: What is the result of the following code?

Answer: The output of the code will be

x is greater

.

Explanation: The code checks if

x

is greater than or less than

y

using the

if-else if-else

statement. If

x > y

, it sets the result variable to "x is greater". If

x < y

, it sets the

result

variable to "y is greater". If x and y are equal

Loop-de-Loop: A Whirlwind Tour of C++ Loops

Greetings, valiant coders! Buckle up and hold on tight, as we embark on a thrilling ride through the fantastical world of C++ loops. You'll encounter mesmerizing loops of all shapes and sizes, as we venture deep into the realm of while loops, for loops, and for each loops. Prepare to be amazed, as these powerful tools will help you tame the wildest coding challenges, and make even the most repetitive tasks a breeze!

First on our grand tour, we'll explore the enigmatic while loop. A creature of habit, the while loop has an insatiable appetite for repetition, chomping away at code blocks as long as its condition remains true. Behold its magnificent structure:

Next, we'll dive into the mystical world of the for loop. This wondrous loop is a multitasker extraordinaire, with the power to initialize, test, and update all in a single, elegant line of code. Witness the splendor of the for loop:

Not to be outdone, the for each loop makes its grand entrance. This loop is the epitome of grace and simplicity, effortlessly gliding through every element in a range or container, bestowing its magic touch upon each one. Behold the enchanting for each loop:

Together, these loops form a formidable trio, ready to conquer any coding challenge that dares cross their path. Whether you're tallying up the number of goblins vanquished, keeping track of spell ingredients, or calculating the trajectory of a rogue asteroid, loops have got you covered.

Now, go forth and wield the awesome power of loops! May your code flow effortlessly, and may the loop-de-loop guide you to coding mastery!

Continue and Break Statements in Loops

In C++ loops, the

continue

and

break

statements are used to control the flow of execution within the loop. They allow you to fine-tune how your loops process the data and help you optimize your code for specific scenarios.

Continue Statement

The continue statement is used to skip the remainder of the current iteration and immediately proceed to the next iteration of the loop. When the continue statement is encountered, the program stops executing the remaining statements within the loop body and jumps to the loop condition to determine whether the loop should continue or not.

This is particularly useful when you need to skip certain elements or perform specific actions only for some elements in a sequence. Example of continue statement:

In this example, the continue statement skips even numbers, and the output will be:

1 3 5 7 9

.

The

break

statement, on the other hand, is used to exit the loop entirely, regardless of whether the loop condition is still true. When a

break

statement is encountered, the program immediately stops executing the loop and jumps to the statement that follows the loop.

This is useful when you want to exit the loop prematurely upon meeting a specific condition, such as finding the desired element in a search operation or stopping the loop when an error occurs. Example of

break

statement:

In this example, the loop stops when the target value (5) is found, and the output will be:

Found target: 5

.

The

continue

and

break

statements are powerful tools for controlling the flow of execution within loops in C++. The

continue

statement allows you to skip the current iteration and proceed to the next one, while the

break

statement enables you to exit the loop entirely. Understanding when and how to use these statements will help you write more efficient and optimized code.

Problem

Greetings, fellow milk-maneuvering aficionados! Today, we are diving into a milk-filled adventure with our favorite farmer, John, and his two milking barns. Let's churn through the details of this creamy conundrum.

Farmer John has two milking barns, and each one is equipped with a 1000-gallon milk tank and a storage closet containing 10 different-sized buckets. He absolutely loves his daily milk-carrying workout routine!

From Tuesday to Friday, Farmer John follows a milk-moving schedule. He begins by alternating between the barns, first taking a bucket, then filling it, and subsequently transferring the milk to the other barn's tank. After completing the transfer, he leaves the bucket behind in that barn. This process is repeated throughout the week, as Farmer John dutifully carries out his milk-transfer ritual.

At the end of the week, specifically on Friday, Farmer John measures the milk in the first barn's tank. Our task is to determine how many possible different readings he could see. By taking into account his milk-moving schedule and the varying bucket sizes, we can calculate the various outcomes for the milk level in the first barn's tank.

So, milk enthusiasts, it's time to put on your dairy-detective hats and help Farmer John make sense of this delightful dairy dilemma. Together, we'll unravel the mystery of the marvelous milking mayhem and find out just how much milk Farmer John has been hauling back and forth!

Analyze

Dear milk mavens, let's put our analytical minds to work and delve into this milky mystery. Here's how we'll approach Farmer John's Marvelous Milking Mayhem:

First, it is essential to understand the milk transfer process that Farmer John follows. Since he uses 10 different-sized buckets and transfers milk four times during the week (from Tuesday to Friday), we have to consider that he can use the same bucket more than once or different buckets each time. Our objective is to figure out all the possible combinations of bucket usage during his milk-carrying workout.

Second, we need to evaluate the milk-swapping routine in order to accurately track the milk flow between the two barns. Each day, Farmer John takes a bucket, fills it, moves the milk to the other barn, and leaves the bucket behind. We will analyze the possible bucket combinations on each day and how they impact the final measurement on Friday.

Lastly, once we have a solid understanding of the milk-transfer process and potential bucket combinations, we can calculate the possible outcomes. It is time to determine the various readings Farmer John could see on Friday when he measures the milk in the first barn's tank. Get ready to unleash your inner milk mathematician!

So, fellow dairy detectives, let's sharpen our pencils, polish our calculators, and dig into this delectable dairy dilemma. With our analytical prowess and passion for all things milk, we'll solve Farmer John's Marvelous Milking Mayhem and uncover the true potential of his milk-carrying escapades!

Solution

Exercises: Loop-de-Loop: A Whirlwind Tour of C++ Loops

1. Question: What are the three types of loops in C++?

Answer: The three types of loops in C++ are:

```
for loop
while loop
do-while loop
```

Explanation: Loops are used to repeatedly execute a block of code until a specific condition is met. The

for

loop is used when the number of iterations is known, the

while

loop is used when the loop should continue as long as a given condition is

true

, and the

do-while

loop is used when the loop should execute at least once and continue as long as a given condition is

true

.

2. Question: Read the following code and determine its output:

Answer: The output of the code will be:

Explanation: The code uses a

for

loop to iterate from 1 to 5 (inclusive), printing the value of the loop variable

i

on each iteration.

3. Question: Write a C++ code snippet that reads a positive integer n from the user and calculates the factorial of

n

(n!) using a
while
loop.

Answer:

Explanation: In this example, we declare an

int

variable

n

and read its value from the user using

cin

. We then use a

while

loop to calculate the factorial of

n

and store the result in the

factorial

variable. Finally, we display the calculated factorial.

4. Question: What is the purpose of the
   break
   statement in C++ loops?

Answer: The

break

statement is used to exit a loop prematurely, stopping its execution immediately.

Explanation: The

break

statement can be used inside a loop (for, while, or do-while) to immediately exit the loop when a certain condition is met. It is useful for cases when the loop should stop before the loop condition is false or before completing all iterations.

5.   Question: What is the result of the following code?

Answer: The output of the code will be

Sum: 55

.

Explanation: The code uses a

while

loop to iterate from 1 to 10 (inclusive) and calculates the sum of all numbers from 1 to 10. The loop variable i is incremented on each iteration, and the value of i is added to the

sum

variable. After the loop is finished, the program displays the calculated sum, which is 55.

6. Question: What is a nested loop, and when is it used in C++?

Answer: A nested loop is a loop placed inside another loop. Nested loops are used when you need to perform a set of operations for each element in a sequence while also iterating through another sequence.

Explanation: Nested loops can be used for tasks that require iterating through multiple dimensions, such as processing matrices or multi-dimensional arrays, or when the number of iterations in an inner loop depends on the current value of the outer loop.

7. Question: Read the following code and determine its output:

Answer: The output of the code will be:

Explanation: The code uses two nested

for

loops to print a pattern of asterisks. The outer loop iterates three times, and for each iteration, the inner loop iterates i times, printing an asterisk. This results in a triangle pattern of asterisks.

8. Question: Write a C++ code snippet that reads a positive integer n from the user and prints a

pattern of numbers in the shape of an inverted triangle, like the following example for

n = 5

:

Answer:

Explanation: In this example, we declare an

int

variable n and read its value from the user using

cin

. We then use nested

for

loops to print the inverted triangle pattern of numbers. The outer loop iterates from n to 1 (inclusive), and the inner loop iterates from the current value of

i

down to

1

, printing the value of

j

on each iteration.

9. Question: What is the purpose of the

continue
statement in C++ loops, and how does it differ from the
break
statement?

Answer: The

continue

statement is used to skip the rest of the current iteration of a loop and move on to the next iteration. It differs from the

break

statement, which exits the loop entirely.

Explanation: The

continue

statement can be used inside a loop (for, while, or do-while) to skip the rest of the current iteration and proceed to the next iteration without executing the remaining statements in the loop body. Unlike the break statement, the continue statement does not exit the loop entirely; it only skips the current iteration.

10. Question: Read the following code and determine its output:

Answer: The output of the code will be:

Explanation: The code uses a

for

loop to iterate from 1 to 5.

C++ Data Structure Saga: Embark on a Quest for Code Conquest"

Hark, noble coders! Gather 'round the binary bonfire, as we regale you with the epic saga of C++ data structures. In a realm where complexity reigns, and information teems, the heroes of code must forge order from chaos. Enter the mighty data structures, forged in the fires of C++ to wield the power of organization!

Fear not, intrepid coders, for data structures are your steadfast allies, ready to aid you in your quest to vanquish the forces of disarray. Whether you're traversing treacherous arrays, unlocking the mysteries of maps and sets, or structuring your own custom data types, these valiant warriors of code shall stand by your side.

In the C++ kingdom, data structures come in many forms, each with their unique strengths and weaknesses:

1. **Arrays**: The trusty foot soldiers of the data realm, marching in strict formation to hold the line against disorder.
2. **Vectors**: Swift and nimble, these dynamic arrays adapt to the ever-changing tides of battle.
3. **Maps and Sets**: The cunning tacticians of the data world, organizing their troops with key-value pairs and set-theory prowess.

4. **Pair**: The dynamic duo of data, combining two disparate elements in a single, cohesive bond. Unbreakable in their unity, they stand as a testament to the power of partnership.
5. **Structs**: Architects of custom data types, these versatile builders can craft intricate edifices to suit any purpose.
6. **Queue**: The disciplined guardians of order, these noble structures maintain a strict First-In-First-Out (FIFO) policy. They ensure that no element can jump the line, and justice prevails for all.
7. **Stack**: Balancing on the edge of chaos, these agile warriors employ a Last-In-First-Out (LIFO) strategy. Their swift and precise actions topple the towers of disorder one block at a time.
8. **Graph**: The grand architects of connections, these interwoven structures create a vast, intricate network of nodes and edges. Their boundless reach spans the farthest corners of the coding realm, linking all in a majestic tapestry of information.

As you journey through the enchanted lands of C++ data structures, you shall encounter puzzles and riddles most arcane, but fear not! For with the power of geek, the wisdom of the professional, and the hearty laughter of humor, you shall conquer the challenges that lie ahead.

So, hoist your coding flagons high and prepare to embark on the grand adventure of C++ data structures. Together, we shall forge a new era of order and organization, and bring forth a golden age of code conquest!

C++ Arrays: The Epic Saga of Fixed-Size Data Warriors

Once upon a time in the mystical land of C++, there was an ancient order of warriors known as the Arrays. These valiant data defenders were renowned for their unwavering dedication to holding their ground, no matter the challenge. In this enchanted realm, the Arrays possess the unparalleled ability to store multiple elements of the same data type in a fixed-size, sequential manner. Let us embark on an epic journey to unveil the secrets of the C++ Arrays!

Gather 'round, noble coders, as we spin the tale of the Array declaration:

Behold the Array in all its glory, a battalion of five brave integers, standing shoulder-to-shoulder, ready for battle. The tale begins with

int

, the noble data type that the Array has sworn to protect. The number within the square brackets

[5]

defines the size of the army, indicating the maximum number of warriors it can accommodate. Finally, the curly braces

{}

enshrine the initial values of the valiant soldiers.

Now, let us witness the might of the Array in action:

By invoking the power of the zero-based index within the square brackets, we can call upon any member of the Array to perform their noble duties. In this enchanted incantation, the first warrior (

mightyWarriors[0]

) and the last warrior (

mightyWarriors[4]

) heed the call to reveal their values: 3 and 42, respectively.

But lo, a cautionary tale must be told! Arrays are formidable, yet they possess an unyielding nature. Once the size of an Array is declared, it cannot be changed, lest the very fabric of the C++ realm unravels. Tread carefully, dear coders, for attempting to summon a warrior beyond the boundaries of the Array shall unleash the dreaded Undefined Behavior.

And thus concludes the epic saga of the C++ Arrays. With their unwavering devotion to duty, they stand as a testament to the power of fixed-size data warriors. May your coding quests be ever triumphant, guided by the wisdom of the geek, the professionalism of the sage, and the levity of the jester!

1. Question: What is an array in C++, and why are arrays useful?

Answer: An array is a fixed-size, contiguous block of memory that stores multiple elements of the same data type. Arrays are useful for organizing and managing large amounts of data efficiently.

Explanation: Arrays provide a way to store multiple values of the same data type in a single variable, making it easier to work with and manipulate large sets of data. They are particularly useful when you need to perform operations on a sequence of elements, such as sorting or searching.

2. Question: How do you declare an array in C++?

Answer: To declare an array in C++, you specify the data type, followed by the array name, and then the size of the array in square brackets. For example:

int myArray[10]

;

Explanation: In this example, we declare an array named

myArray

with a size of 10 elements, all of which are of type int.

3. Question: How do you access elements of an array in C++?

Answer: You access elements of an array by using the array name followed by an index in square brackets. For example: myArray[3]

Explanation: In this example, we access the fourth element (since C++ uses zero-based indexing) of the myArray array.

4. Question: What is the range of valid indices for an array of size n in C++?

Answer: The range of valid indices for an array of size n is 0 to n-1.

Explanation: C++ uses zero-based indexing, so the first element of an array is at index 0, and the last element is at index n-1.

5. Question: Read the following code and determine its output:

Answer: The output of the code will be 12.

Explanation: The code accesses the second element of the array

arr

(which is 4) and the fourth element (which is 8), then adds them together, resulting in the output 12.

6. Question: Write a C++ code snippet that reads a positive integer

n

from the user, creates an array of size n, fills it with the first n even numbers, and then prints the sum of the array's elements.

Answer:

Explanation: In this example, we declare an

int

variable

n

, read its value from the user using

cin

, and then create an array of size

n

. We then use a

for

loop to fill the array with the first

n

even numbers and calculate the sum at the same time. Finally, we print the sum of the array's elements.

7. Question: What is the difference between a one-dimensional array and a two-dimensional array in C++?

Answer: A one-dimensional array stores elements in a single row or column, while a two-dimensional array

C++ Vectors: The Shape-Shifting Magicians of Data Storage

In the mystical realm of C++, where valiant data warriors defend the sanctity of code, a new breed of sorcerers has emerged: the enigmatic Vectors. These shape-shifting magicians are masters of adaptability, capable of resizing their storage containers with the fluidity of a swirling potion. Let us delve into the arcane secrets of the C++ Vectors and unleash their true power!

With a dramatic flourish, we conjure the Vector declaration:

Behold the Vector's shimmering incantation, which begins with

#include

, the sacred scroll from which the Vector's power is drawn. The vector

summons the Vector and binds it to the noble

int

data type, transforming it into a conduit for integers. The curly braces

{}

imbue the Vector with its initial values, granting it the power to store elements in a dynamic and flexible manner.

Now, witness the Vector's shape-shifting magic in action:

The

push_back()

spell enchants the Vector, allowing it to expand its size and accommodate new elements. In this case, the number 24 joins the ranks of the enchantedNumbers. Conversely, the

pop_back()

incantation gracefully reduces the size of the Vector, removing the last element with a subtle puff of smoke.

Behold the Vector's spellbinding versatility:

The

size()

spell reveals the current size of the Vector, illuminating the number of elements contained within its mystical bounds. The enchanting powers of the zero-based index grant us the ability to access any element within the Vector, just as we would with their more rigid brethren, the Arrays.

And thus, the magical tale of the C++ Vectors unfolds. Embrace their shape-shifting powers, and let your coding adventures be filled with the wisdom of the geek, the elegance of the professional, and the laughter of the jesters. May the Vectors guide you through the ever-changing landscape of data storage!

Example: 2015 December Contest, Bronze Problem 2. Speeding Ticket

Problem

Bessie, the rebellious cow, has taken Farmer John's tractor for a wild 100-mile joyride, ending in a police officer issuing her tickets for multiple violations. Although she accepts two of the charges, Bessie's skeptical about the speeding ticket and wants to verify if she exceeded the speed limit during her adventure.

The road consists of N segments, each with a distinct length in miles and a speed limit ranging from 1 to 100 miles per hour. The total length of all N segments equals 100 miles. For instance, the road might start with a 45-mile segment at a 70 mph speed limit, followed by a 55-mile segment at a 60 mph speed limit.

Bessie's journey is also divided into M segments, each having a specific length in miles and a speed. The sum of all M segments' lengths is 100 miles. Farmer John's tractor can reach a top speed of 100 mph.

Considering the given information, we aim to determine the maximum amount Bessie exceeded the speed limit at any point during her joyride. Let's buckle up and dive into this bovine-speeding conundrum!

Analyze

As we embark on this joyride with Bessie, let's take a smarter route to analyze the problem using two vectors, one to store her speeds and another to store the speed limits of each road segment. This approach will help us simplify the solution and keep up with Bessie's antics.

First, we create two vectors:

bessieSpeeds

and

speedLimits

. We'll populate

bessieSpeeds

with the speeds Bessie travels during each of her M segments, and

speedLimits

with the speed limits of each N road segment. Now, we have a clear view of Bessie's journey and the road's constraints.

Next, we'll iterate through both vectors simultaneously, comparing Bessie's speed to the speed limit at each mile of her journey. To do this, we can use two nested loops. The outer loop will traverse through

speedLimits

, and the inner loop will go through

bessieSpeeds

. While iterating, we'll keep track of the remaining length of each segment to ensure we compare the right speed values.

During the comparison, we'll calculate the speed difference between Bessie's speed and the speed limit. If Bessie's speed is greater, we'll note the difference and update the maximum amount she exceeded the speed limit.

At the end of this rollercoaster ride, we'll have the maximum amount Bessie exceeded the speed limit during her journey.

Solution

Exercises: C++ Vectors: The Shape-Shifting Magicians of Data Storage

1. Question: What is a vector in C++, and how does it differ from an array?

Answer: A vector is a dynamic, resizable array-like container provided by the C++ Standard Library. Unlike arrays, vectors can be resized during runtime, and their size can be changed as elements are added or removed.

Explanation: Vectors provide more flexibility compared to arrays, as they can be resized and offer various built-in functions to manage elements more easily.

2. Question: How do you include the necessary library to use
    vectors
    in C++?

Answer: To use vectors in C++, you must include the

header. For example:

#include

Explanation: The

header is part of the C++ Standard Library and provides the necessary definitions for the vector class template.

3. Question: How do you declare and initialize a vector in C++?

Answer: To declare and initialize a vector, you specify the vector keyword, followed by the data type in angle brackets, and then the vector name. You can optionally provide an initializer list to set the initial elements. For example:

vector myVector = {1, 2, 3, 4};

Explanation: In this example, we declare a vector named myVector that stores int elements and initializes it with the elements 1, 2, 3, and 4.

4. Question: How do you access elements of a vector in C++?

Answer: You can access elements of a vector using the [] operator with an index or by using the

at()

member function. For example:

myVector[1]

or

myVector.at(1)

Explanation: In both examples, we access the second element (since C++ uses zero-based indexing) of the

myVector

vector.

5. Question: What is the range of valid indices for a vector of size n in C++?

Answer: The range of valid indices for a vector of size n is 0 to n-1.

Explanation: Like arrays, C++ vectors use zero-based indexing, so the first element of a vector is at index 0, and the last element is at index n-1.

6. Question: Read the following code and determine its output:

Answer: The output of the code will be 12.

Explanation: The code accesses the second element of the vector

vec

(which is 4) and the fourth element (which is 8), then adds them together, resulting in the output 12.

7. Question: Write a C++ code snippet that reads a positive integer n from the user, creates a vector of size n, fills it with the first n even numbers, and then prints the sum of the vector's elements.

Answer:

C++ Maps: Charting the Labyrinthine Key-Value Universe

Deep within the cryptic cosmos of C++ lies a fantastical dimension, a world where pairs of data are bound together in a celestial dance: the Map. This realm of key-value connections is guarded by the wise and witty cartographers who chart the constellations of data, illuminating the path to programming enlightenment. Join us, brave adventurer, as we traverse the labyrinthine domain of the C++ Maps!

To summon the Map, chant the sacred incantation:

With the #include

invocation, we unlock the arcane Map scroll, bestowing upon us the power to create the key-value cosmos. The

map<string, int>

beckons the Map and binds it to the noble data types

string

and

int

, forging a celestial bond between the key and the value.

Now, let us populate our Map with astral entities:

The Map's key, a

string

in this case, acts as a celestial gatekeeper, ushering in the corresponding value, an

int

. This mystical pairing forms the backbone of the C++ Map, creating a universe of interconnected data.

Explore the cosmic wonders of the Map's astral capabilities:

By invoking the key, we unlock the secrets of the corresponding value, illuminating the Map's labyrinthine pathways. The

erase()

incantation banishes a key-value pair from the celestial plane, as if it never existed.

map

and

unordered_map

are both associative containers in C++ that store key-value pairs, allowing you to efficiently retrieve a value based on its corresponding key. However, they have different underlying implementations and characteristics, which affect their performance and usage scenarios.

map

is typically implemented as a balanced binary search tree (usually a red-black tree), which maintains the key-value pairs sorted by their keys. Due to its sorted nature, operations like insertion, deletion, and searching take O(log n) time complexity, where n is the number of elements in the map. Since the elements are ordered, you can easily perform operations that require sorted data, such as iterating through the map in a specific order or finding the closest key to a given value.

unordered_map

is implemented as a hash table, which provides average-case constant-time complexity (O(1)) for insertion, deletion, and searching. However, in the worst case, these operations can take up to O(n) time complexity due to hash collisions. Unlike

map

, the elements in an

unordered_map

are not ordered, so you cannot perform operations that rely on a specific ordering of keys.

When deciding whether to use

map

or

unordered_map

, consider the following factors:

1. Ordering requirement: If you need to maintain the elements in a sorted order, use map. If the order of the elements is not important, use unordered_map for faster average-case performance.
2. Performance: If you expect constant-time complexity for most operations and can handle the potential worst-case performance, use unordered_map. If you prefer more predictable and balanced performance, use map.
3. Hash function: unordered_map relies on a hash function to distribute the keys evenly. If you have custom key types, you need to provide a suitable hash function for your key type. If creating an efficient hash function is challenging or not possible, use map, which only requires a comparison function for the keys.

In summary, choose map if you need sorted data or balanced performance, and use unordered_map if you want faster average-case performance and don't require ordering.

And so, our celestial expedition through the C++ Maps draws to a close. As you navigate the twisting pathways of key-value connections, remember the lessons of the geek, the poise of the professional, and the laughter of the jesters. May your programming journey be guided by the stars!

Example: 2019 December Contest, Bronze Problem 3. Livestock Lineup

Problem

Farmer John milks his 8 dairy cows daily: Bessie, Buttercup, Belinda, Beatrice, Bella, Blue, Betsy, and Sue. These cows can be quite finicky and require Farmer John to follow N constraints ($1 <= N <= 7$) when milking them. Each constraint states that "X must be milked beside Y," meaning cow X must appear in the milking order directly after cow Y or directly before cow Y.

Farmer John needs help to determine an ordering of his cows that satisfies all these constraints. It's guaranteed that a valid ordering is always possible. If multiple orderings work, output the one that is alphabetically first. In other words, the first cow should have the lowest alphabetical name among all possible cows that could appear first in any valid ordering. Among all orderings starting with the same alphabetically-first cow, the second cow should be alphabetically lowest among all possible valid orderings, and so on.

Analyze

Ah, the life of a farmer dealing with picky cows! Let's break down this utterly (or should I say udderly)

confusing milking order problem to make it more digestible, just like how cows break down their food through rumination.

First, let's clarify the problem statement: Farmer John has 8 cows, and they are quite particular about their milking order. There are N constraints given, which dictate that cow X must be milked either directly before or directly after cow Y.

The key to solving this problem is finding an ordering of cows that satisfies all N constraints. If there are multiple valid orderings, we need to return the one that is alphabetically first.

Now, let's moo-ve to the analysis part. Since there are only 8 cows, we can use a depth-first search (DFS) algorithm to explore all possible orderings of cows. We can represent the constraints as a graph where each cow is a node and an edge between two nodes indicates the constraint between those cows.

Starting with an empty path, we'll apply DFS to traverse the graph, extending the path by adding adjacent cows that haven't been visited yet. At each step, we'll check if the path satisfies the constraints. If the path becomes invalid, we backtrack and try other possibilities. If we reach the end of the path, it means we found a valid ordering.

As we are searching for the alphabetically first ordering, we'll explore nodes (cows) in alphabetical order during DFS. This ensures that we find the lexicographically smallest solution.

Once we find a valid ordering, we can be sure it's the alphabetically first one due to our DFS traversal strategy. And there you have it! Farmer John can now milk his cows happily in their preferred order, and the cows can continue being their usual picky selves.

Solution

1. What is a hash map in C++?

Answer: A hash map, also known as an unordered map in C++, is a container that stores key-value pairs, where each key is associated with a unique value. It allows for fast retrieval, insertion, and deletion of elements based on their keys, as it uses a hash function to map the keys to indices in the underlying data structure.

2. Which header file should be included to use unordered_map in C++?

Answer: To use unordered_map in C++, you need to include the

header file.

3. How do you declare an

unordered_map
with
int
as the key and
string
as the value?

Answer: To declare an

unordered_map

with

int

as the key and

string

as the value, use the following syntax:

4. How do you insert a key-value pair into an unordered_map?

Answer: You can insert a key-value pair into an unordered_map using the

insert()

function or the [] operator. For example:

5. Write a code snippet that counts the frequency of words in a vector of strings using an unordered_map.

Answer:

6. How do you access the value associated with a given key in an unordered_map?

Answer: You can access the value associated with a given key in an unordered_map using the [] operator or the at() function. For example:

7. How do you check if a key exists in an unordered_map?

Answer: You can check if a key exists in an unordered_map using the find() function. If the key is not present in the map, the find() function returns an iterator pointing to the end() of the map. For example:

8. How do you remove an element from an unordered_map given its key?

Answer: You can remove an element from an unordered_map given its key using the erase() function. For example:

C++ Sets: The Elite Ensemble of Unique Elements

Greetings, valiant code warriors! As you embark on your quest through the enchanted realm of C++, it's time to uncover the power of a truly magical artifact: the Set. This wondrous container conjures an army of unique elements, ensuring that no duplicates may enter its sanctum. Join us as we delve into the arcane arts of C++ Sets and discover their elite secrets.

To wield the power of the Set, you must first recite the ancient incantation:

With the

#include

spell, we unseal the mystical tome of Sets, granting us the ability to summon an elite assembly of distinct integers – the

spellbindingSorcerers

.

Now, let us perform a divine ritual to fill our Set with hallowed elements:

Behold! The Set's sacred aura repels any duplicates, maintaining its divine purity. Our

spellbindingSorcerers

Set now contains only the unique elements 42 and 1337, with the second attempt to insert 42 being vanquished by the Set's impenetrable enchantment.

To traverse the sacred domain of the Set, we shall invoke the powers of the Iterator:

Armed with the Iterator's foresight, we venture through the hallowed halls of the Set, witnessing the elite assembly of unique elements in all their resplendent glory.

set

and

unordered_set

are both container classes in C++ that store unique elements, similar to how

map

and

unordered_map

store key-value pairs. The main difference is that sets store only keys, whereas maps store both keys and their corresponding values. Sets are useful when you need to keep track of unique elements without the need for associated values.

set

is typically implemented as a balanced binary search tree (usually a red-black tree), which maintains the elements in a sorted order. Operations like insertion, deletion, and searching take O(log n) time complexity, where n is the number of elements in the set. Since the elements are ordered, you can easily perform operations that require sorted data, such as iterating through the set in a specific order or finding the closest element to a given value.

unordered_set

is implemented as a hash table, which provides average-case constant-time complexity (O(1)) for insertion, deletion, and searching. However, in the worst case, these operations can take up to O(n) time complexity due to hash collisions. Unlike set, the elements in an

unordered_set

are not ordered, so you cannot perform operations that rely on a specific ordering of elements.

When deciding whether to use

set

or

unordered_set

, consider the following factors:

1. Ordering requirement: If you need to maintain the elements in a sorted order, use set. If the order of the elements is not important, use unordered_set for faster average-case performance.

2. Performance: If you expect constant-time complexity for most operations and can handle the potential worst-case performance, use unordered_set. If you prefer more predictable and balanced performance, use set.

3. Hash function: unordered_set relies on a hash function to distribute the keys evenly. If you have custom key types, you need to provide a

suitable hash function for your key type. If creating an efficient hash function is challenging or not possible, use set, which only requires a comparison function for the keys.

In summary, choose set if you need sorted data or balanced performance, and use unordered_set if you want faster average-case performance and don't require ordering. This choice is similar to the one between map and unordered_map, but for sets, you only store and manage keys without associated values.

And so, our exhilarating journey through the magical world of C++ Sets comes to a close. With the wisdom of the geek, the focus of the professional, and the humor that keeps our spirits high, you shall wield the power of Sets to forge a triumphant path through the enchanted realm of C++ programming. Go forth, and let the Sets guide you to victory!

Exercises: C++ Sets: The Elite Ensemble of Unique Elements

1. What is a hash set in C++?

Answer: A hash set, also known as an unordered_set in C++, is a container that stores unique elements in no particular order. It allows for fast retrieval, insertion, and deletion of elements, as it uses a hash function to map the elements to indices in the underlying data structure.

2. Which header file should be included to use unordered_set in C++?

Answer: To use unordered_set in C++, you need to include the header file.

3. How do you declare an unordered_set with int as the element type?

Answer: To declare an unordered_set with int as the element type, use the following syntax:

4. How do you insert an element into an unordered_set?

Answer: You can insert an element into an unordered_set using the insert() function. For example:

5. Write a code snippet that removes duplicate elements from a vector of integers using an unordered_set.

Answer:

6. How do you check if an element exists in an unordered_set?

Answer: You can check if an element exists in an unordered_set using the find() function. If the element is not present in the set, the find() function returns an iterator pointing to the end() of the set. For example:

7. How do you remove an element from an unordered_set?

Answer: You can remove an element from an unordered_set using the erase() function. For example:

8. How do you find the number of elements in an unordered_set?

Answer: You can find the number of elements in an

unordered_set

using the

size()

function. For example:

9. Can an unordered_set contain duplicate elements?

Answer: No, an unordered_set cannot contain duplicate elements. Each element in an unordered_set is unique.

10 Write a code snippet that finds the intersection of two unordered_sets of integers.

Answer:

C++ Pairs: The Dynamic Duo of Data

Behold! A mythical beast roams the hallowed halls of C++ lore: the Pair. This enigmatic entity fuses two distinct data types in a cosmic union, forming a syntactic symbiosis that'll leave you starstruck. So, fellow code conjurer, let us embark on a thrilling adventure, unraveling the duality of C++ Pairs and harnessing their programming prowess.

To summon the Pair, you must utter the sacred incantation:

By invoking the

#include

charm, we unlock the fabled Pair scroll, empowering us to forge a mighty bond between two disparate data types:

string

and

int

. With the Pair's power now in our grasp, we can create the

heroicHeterodyad

.

To breathe life into our Pair, we must perform the arcane ritual:

The

make_pair()

spell weaves together the two data types, "Merlin" and 777, in a mystical union, bestowing them with the divine essence of the Pair.

Now, let us unveil the secrets of the Pair's duality:

In the twilight of the C++ realm, the

.first

and

.second

enchantments illuminate the two faces of the Pair, revealing the sublime synergy of its dual nature.

And so, dear adventurer, our exhilarating escapade through the C++ Pairs comes to an end. As you harness the duality of the Pair, may you always remember the geek's wisdom, the professional's poise, and the humor that sparks joy in the heart of the coder. With the Pair by your side, you shall conquer the programming cosmos!

Exercises: C++ Pairs: The Dynamic Duo of Data

1. What is a pair in C++?

Answer: A pair in C++ is a simple container that stores two elements of potentially different types.

Pairs are useful when you need to store two related values together as a single entity.

2. Which header file should be included to use pair in C++?

Answer: To use pair in C++, you need to include the

header file.

3. How do you declare a pair with int as the first
    element and string as the second element?

Answer: To declare a pair with int as the

first

element and string as the second element, use the following syntax:

4. How do you assign values to the elements of a pair?

Answer: You can assign values to the elements of a pair using the

first

and second member variables. For example:

5. Write a code snippet that creates a vector of pairs, where each pair contains an integer and its square.

Answer:

6. How can you create a pair using the make_pair()
    function?

Answer: You can create a pair using the

make_pair()

function by providing the two values as arguments. The function will return a pair with the specified values. For example:

7. How do you access the first and second elements of a pair?

Answer: You can access the first and second elements of a pair using the first and second member variables. For example:

8. Can a pair be used as a key in an unordered_map?

Answer: No, a pair cannot be used as a key in an unordered_map directly because pairs do not have a predefined hash function. However, you can use a pair as a key in a map since map uses a comparison function instead of a hash function.

9. Write a code snippet that sorts a vector of pairs based on the second element in each pair.

Answer:

C++ Structs: Assembling the Avengers of Data Types

Hear ye, hear ye, fellow code slingers! Gather round, for today we embark on an epic quest to unite the mightiest of data types within the hallowed halls of C++ Structs. As we forge this legendary alliance, we'll create custom data structures, bringing together an assortment of data types under a single banner, much like the Avengers themselves. So, strap on your armor, grab your enchanted keyboard, and let's dive into the fantastical world of Structs!

To summon a Struct, one must recite the ancient incantation known as the Struct Declaration:

Behold, as we conjure forth a majestic

Wizard

Struct, assembling the valiant heroes of

string

,

int

, and

double

. This formidable alliance of data types bands together under the

Wizard

banner, each member retaining their individual powers – the

name

,

level

, and

mana

of our conjured wizards.

Now, let us breathe life into our

Wizard

Struct, creating an instance of this enchanted entity:

In a burst of cosmic energy, we forge a legendary instance of our

Wizard

Struct, crafting the one and only Gandalf the Grey, complete with his name, level, and mana. The

gandalf

variable shall henceforth bear the hallowed mark of the

Wizard

Struct.

With our mighty wizard at our side, we may now harness the power of his arcane attributes:

As we invoke the celestial wisdom of

gandalf

, we witness the awe-inspiring union of data types within our

Wizard

Struct, a testament to the boundless possibilities that await us in the enchanted realm of C++ programming.

C++

struct

and

class

have several similarities, as both are user-defined data types that can group together variables of different data types under a single name. Here are some of the key similarities:

1. Both
    struct
    and
    class

can contain data members (variables) and member functions (methods).

2. They can both have constructors and destructors.

3. Inheritance can be used with both

struct

and

class

.

4. They both support access specifiers (public, private, and protected).

The primary difference between

struct

and

class

lies in their default access levels. For a

struct

, the default access level is

public

, whereas for a

class

, it's

private

. This difference has implications for the default accessibility of member variables and inherited classes.

In practice,

class

is often favored in general programming because it promotes encapsulation, which is a key principle of object-oriented programming. By default,

class

members are private, which means they can only be accessed by the class's member functions. This helps maintain the integrity of the data and makes it easier to reason about the behavior of the class, as well as making it easier to modify the class without affecting the rest of the codebase.

However, in competitive programming and coding challenges, the primary focus is often on writing code quickly and efficiently, rather than adhering to strict object-oriented programming principles. In these situations, using a

struct

can be advantageous due to its default public access level, which allows for easier and faster access to its members without the need for getter and setter functions. Moreover, when working with simple data structures where encapsulation is not a significant concern, using a

struct

can lead to more concise and easily understandable code.

In summary, the choice between

struct

and

class

depends on the context and the goals of the code being written. For general programming and when adhering to object-oriented principles, using a

class

is usually the preferred choice. In competitive programming and coding challenges, where the focus is on speed and efficiency, a

struct

might be more convenient and suitable.

And thus, we conclude our whirlwind adventure through the fantastical world of C++ Structs. Armed with the geek's knowledge, the professional's focus, and the humor that keeps us all going, you are now ready to wield the power of Structs and forge your own legendary alliances in the ever-expanding universe of C++!

Example: 2023 January Contest, Bronze Problem 2. Air Cownditioning II

Problem

It's been a blazing hot summer at Farmer John's farm, and his cows are feeling the heat. To keep his bovine buddies cool, Farmer John decides to invest in some air conditioners for their barn.

The barn has N cows ($1 <= N <= 20$) and 100 stalls in a row, each occupied by a unique cow. Cow i lives in the range of stalls from s_i to t_i, and requires cooling of c_i units to stay comfortable.

Farmer John has M air conditioners ($1 <= M <= 10$), each with a cost m_i to operate ($1 <= m_i <= 1000$). Air conditioner i cools the stalls from a_i to b_i, decreasing the temperature by p_i units ($1 <= p_i <= 10^6$). The cooling ranges of air conditioners may overlap.

Being a frugal farmer, Farmer John wants to keep his cows comfy without breaking the bank. Our task is to determine the minimum amount he needs to spend on air conditioning to keep all of his cows content. We're guaranteed that all cows will be comfortable if he uses all of his air conditioners.

Time to chill out and analyze this sweltering situation! We can approach this problem by iterating through all possible subsets of air conditioners, checking if each subset can satisfy the cows' cooling requirements. To minimize the cost, we'll calculate the total cost for each valid subset and return the smallest value.

It's essential to consider all subsets since some air conditioners may have overlapping cooling ranges, and we want to find the most cost-efficient combination.

In the end, Farmer John can keep his cows cool and comfortable while saving some moo-lah for other farm expenses.

Analyze

Heatwaves are sweeping across Farmer John's farm, and the cows are in dire need of a chill pill. So, Farmer John decides to go shopping for air conditioners to transform the sizzling barn into a cool cow haven.

The barn houses N cows ($1 <= N <= 20$) and consists of 100 stalls in a row, each hosting a unique cow. Cow i has claimed the stalls in the range from s_i to t_i and demands c_i units of cooling to stay content.

To beat the heat, Farmer John has M air conditioners ($1 <= M <= 10$) at his disposal. Each air conditioner i comes with a price tag m_i ($1 <= m_i <= 1000$) and cools down the stalls from a_i to b_i, offering a refreshing p_i units of temperature reduction ($1 <= p_i <= 10^6$). Keep in mind, the cooling ranges of air conditioners can overlap.

Always on the lookout for a bargain, Farmer John wants to ensure his cows are cool and cozy without spending a fortune. Our mission, should we choose to accept it, is to find the least amount of money he needs to shell out to keep all his cows happy. Thankfully, we're assured that if he utilizes all of his air conditioners, every cow will be comfortable.

So, let's dive into this heated problem and figure out the coolest solution! We can tackle this challenge by iterating through all possible subsets of air conditioners and checking if each subset meets the cows' cooling demands. To minimize the expense, we'll compute the total cost for each valid subset and return the smallest value.

Considering all subsets is crucial because some air conditioners may have overlapping cooling ranges. We're aiming to find the most budget-friendly combination that keeps the cows cool and comfortable.

Once we've found the optimal solution, Farmer John can keep his cows cool as cucumbers while saving some moo-ney for other farm necessities. Time to turn up the AC and bring on the chill vibes!

Solution

Exercises: C++ Structs: Assembling the Avengers of Data Types
1. What is a struct in C++?

Answer: A struct (short for structure) in C++ is a user-defined data type that groups together variables under a single name. It can store multiple variables of different data types, making it easier to organize and manage related data.

2. How do you define a struct in C++?

Answer: To define a

struct

in C++, use the struct keyword, followed by the name of the struct and its member variables enclosed in curly braces. For example:

3. How do you create an instance of a struct?

Answer: To create an instance of a struct, use the struct's name followed by the instance's name. For example:

4. How do you access the member variables of a struct?

Answer: You can access the member variables of a struct using the dot (.) operator. For example:

5. Write a code snippet that defines a struct
Person
with the member variables
name
,
age

, and

address

, and creates an instance of the struct.

Answer:

6.   Can a struct contain a member function?

Answer: Yes, a struct can contain member functions just like a class. The main difference between structs and classes is the default access specifier: it is

public

for structs and

private

for classes.

7.   Can a struct have a constructor?

Answer: Yes, a struct can have a constructor, which is a special member function that initializes the struct's member variables when an instance of the struct is created. For example:

To create an instance of this struct, you can use the following syntax:

8.   Can a struct be used as a key in a map or unordered_map?

Answer: Yes, a struct can be used as a key in a map if you provide a custom comparison function. For unordered_map, you need to provide both a custom hash function and an equality operator for the struct.

9. Write a code snippet that sorts a vector of Person structs by age.

Answer:

This code defines a

Person

struct and a

compare_by_age

function for comparing two

Person

instances by their age. The

main()

function creates a vector of Person instances and sorts them by age using the

compare_by_age

function. Finally, it prints the sorted list of people.

C++ Queues: Form an Orderly Line, Data Types!

Greetings, fellow code enthusiasts! Today, we embark on a riveting journey to the land of C++ Queues, where data types assemble in orderly lines, patiently awaiting their turn to be processed. Prepare to be amazed as we venture into the realm of first-in, first-out (FIFO) data structures. Strap on your coding boots, grab your trusty keyboard, and join us as we delve into the captivating world of Queues!

In C++'s mystical library kingdom, the mighty

bestows upon us the power of the Queue. To harness this magnificent force, we must first pay homage to the sacred header:

With the ancient rite complete, we can now conjure a Queue of valiant integers, ready to serve in the name of FIFO:

Behold, as we raise an army of

nobleNumbers

, an unwavering Queue of integers steadfast in their commitment to FIFO order.

Let's rally the troops and enlist new integers into our Queue:

With the mighty

push()

command, we summon the integers 42, 1337, and 9001 to our cause, each falling in line as they join the

nobleNumbers

Queue.

Now, it's time to reward our most loyal integer, the one who has patiently awaited its turn at the front of the line:

Using the divine

front()

method, we bestow honor upon the first integer in line, revealing its true identity as the noble number 42.

Finally, we must bid farewell to our most faithful integer as it completes its sacred FIFO duty:

With a heavy heart, we invoke the mighty

pop()

command, releasing our venerable integer from the Queue and allowing the next loyal number to step forward.

And so, our thrilling expedition into the world of C++ Queues comes to an end. Now armed with the geek's wisdom, the professional's poise, and a hearty dose of humor, you are prepared to command the power of

Queues and create your own valiant FIFO data structures in the vast realm of C++!

1. What is a queue data structure in C++? Explain its basic operations.

Answer: A queue is a linear data structure in C++ that follows the First-In-First-Out (FIFO) principle. It allows insertion of elements at the back (enqueue) and removal of elements from the front (dequeue). Basic operations include

push()

,

pop()

,

front()

,

back()

,

empty()

, and

size()

.

2. Which header file is required to use the queue container in C++?

Answer: The

header file is required to use the queue container in C++.

3. What is the difference between push() and pop() functions in a queue?

Answer: The

push()

function is used to add an element at the back of the queue, whereas the

pop()

function is used to remove an element from the front of the queue.

4. Write a code snippet that creates a queue of integers, adds the numbers 1 to 5, and then removes and prints the elements until the queue is empty.

5. What will be the output of the following code?

Answer: The output will be 20 30.

6. How can you check if a queue is empty or not?

Answer: You can use the

empty()

function to check if a queue is empty or not. It returns

true

if the queue is empty, otherwise, it returns

false

.

7. Can you use a queue to implement a stack? If yes, explain how.

Answer: Yes, it is possible to implement a stack using two queues. When pushing an element, add it to the non-empty queue. When popping an element, dequeue all but the last element from the non-empty queue and enqueue them into the other queue. Then, dequeue the last element from the non-empty queue. This will be the top of the stack.

8. Write a code snippet to reverse the elements of a queue.
9. What is the time complexity of the push()

and
pop()
operations in a queue?

Answer: The time complexity of both

push()

and

pop()

operations in a queue is O(1).

C++ Stacks: The Tower of Data Power!

Greetings once again, coding aficionados! Today, we embark on yet another thrilling escapade into the enchanting world of C++ data structures. This time, we venture into the realm of Stacks—a towering monument to the might of last-in, first-out (LIFO) organization. Prepare to be dazzled as we ascend the heights of the Stack and unleash the power of reverse order!

In the mystical kingdom of C++ libraries, the revered

bestows upon us the arcane knowledge of the Stack. To harness this awe-inspiring power, we must first pay homage to the sacred header:

With the ancient incantation uttered, we are now free to conjure a Stack of valiant integers, standing tall and proud in the name of LIFO:

Behold, as we erect the

towerOfNumbers

, a magnificent Stack of integers unyielding in their commitment to LIFO order.

Let's now summon the mighty integers and raise our tower to even greater heights:

With the potent

push()

command, we invoke the integers 42, 1337, and 9001 to join our cause, each standing atop the previous one as they form the

towerOfNumbers

Stack.

Now, it's time to honor the noble integer that courageously stands at the summit of our tower:

Using the divine

top()

method, we celebrate the integer at the pinnacle of the Stack, revealing its true identity as the majestic number 9001.

Finally, we must bid adieu to our reigning champion as it completes its sacred LIFO duty:

With a solemn nod, we invoke the powerful

pop()

command, dethroning our esteemed integer from the Stack and allowing the next valiant number to ascend to the summit.

And so, our exhilarating odyssey into the world of C++ Stacks draws to a close. Now armed with the geek's wisdom, the professional's poise, and a hearty dose of humor, you are ready to wield the power of

Stacks and erect your own magnificent LIFO data structures in the vast realm of C++!

1. What is a stack data structure in C++? Explain its basic operations.

Answer: A stack is a linear data structure in C++ that follows the Last-In-First-Out (LIFO) principle. Basic operations include

push()

(inserting an element at the top),

pop()

(removing the top element),

top()

(accessing the top element),

empty()

(checking if the stack is empty), and

size()

(getting the number of elements).

2. Which header file is required to use the stack container in C++?

Answer: The

header file is required to use the stack container in C++.

3. What is the difference between
   push()
   and
   pop()
   functions in a stack?

Answer: The

push()

function is used to add an element at the top of the stack, whereas the

pop()

function is used to remove the top element from the stack.

4. Write a code snippet that creates a stack of integers, pushes the numbers 1 to 5, and then pops and prints the elements until the stack is empty.

5. What will be the output of the following code?

Answer: The output will be 20.

6. How can you check if a stack is empty or not?

Answer: You can use the

empty()

function to check if a stack is empty or not. It returns true

if the stack is empty, otherwise, it returns false

.

7. Can you use a stack to implement a queue? If yes, explain how.

Answer: Yes, it is possible to implement a queue using two stacks. When enqueuing an element, push it onto stack 1. When dequeuing an element, if stack 2 is empty, pop all elements from stack 1 and push them onto stack 2, then pop the top element from stack 2. This will be the front of the queue.

8. Write a code snippet to reverse a string using a stack.
9. What is the time complexity of the push()
and
pop()
operations in a stack?

Answer: The time complexity of both

push()

and

pop()

operations in a stack is O(1).

10. How can you use a stack to evaluate a postfix expression?

Answer: To evaluate a postfix expression using a stack, iterate through the expression. If the current character is an operand, push it onto the stack. If the current character is an operator, pop the top two operands from the stack, perform the operation, and push the result back onto the stack. When the iteration is complete, the stack

The Dynamic Duo - Deque in C++

Welcome, fellow code enthusiasts, to a thrilling adventure through the fantastic world of C++! Today, we will embark on an exciting journey to explore the versatile and powerful "Deque" (pronounced "deck"), a container that can seamlessly transition between a stack and a queue with the same ease as switching between your favorite superhero costumes.

Picture this: you're fighting crime as a superhero coder, and you need a trusty sidekick that can flexibly support your operations. Enter the Deque, a dynamic data structure that is always ready to adapt to your needs. Whether you want to add or remove elements from the front or back, the Deque has got you covered. The Origin Story

In C++, the deque is a part of the standard library and stands for "double-ended queue." It is implemented as a dynamic array that can grow or shrink from both ends, granting it extraordinary powers.

To harness the might of the Deque, you must first include its header file:

Now, let's create a Deque of integers to demonstrate its abilities:

Deque to the Rescue: Queue Mode

The Deque's first superpower is its ability to transform into a queue. When you need to maintain a first-in, first-out (FIFO) order, it's your go-to container. You can easily push elements to the back and pop them from the front.

Behold the mighty Deque, serving up impeccable queue performance!

Deque Strikes Again: Stack Mode

But wait, there's more! Our versatile Deque can also slip into the role of a stack, maintaining a last-in, first-out (LIFO) order. It can push elements to the back and pop them from the back, all with the grace and speed of your favorite superhero.

With the Deque's uncanny ability to switch between a queue and a stack, you'll never have to choose between the two ever again!

Extraordinary Feats of Deque

In addition to its shape-shifting capabilities, the Deque has an array of other powers at its disposal. It can provide you with its current size, check if it's empty, and even clear its contents in the blink of an eye.

The Deque Legacy

And so, our journey through the mystical world of Deque comes to an end. Armed with its incredible versatility and the ability to switch between a queue and a stack, you can now face any coding challenge with confidence.

The Deque is the Swiss Army Knife of the coding world, ever ready to adapt and transform to cater to your algorithmic needs. It's like having a coding genie granting you infinite wishes, limited only by your imagination.

As you venture forth into the unknown realms of coding, remember that the Deque has your back, offering speed, efficiency, and adaptability in a single, elegant package. The Deque may not have a cape or a flashy costume, but it's undoubtedly a silent hero in the world of data structures.

In the annals of C++ history, the Deque will forever be remembered as a steadfast companion to coders far and wide. Whether you're a newbie embarking on your first coding adventure or a seasoned veteran tackling the most complex of problems, the Deque will always be by your side, ready to unleash its powers when called upon.

As you continue to hone your coding skills, remember the lessons of the Deque. Embrace its versatility, and let it guide you in your quest for coding mastery. With the Deque at your side, you can rest assured that you're well-equipped to handle any challenge that comes your way.

In the words of a wise old programmer, "With great power comes great responsibility." Use the Deque wisely, my fellow code warriors, and may the spirit of the Deque be with you, always!

Exercises: The Dynamic Duo - Deque in C++

1. What is a deque in C++ and which header file should be included to use it?

Answer: A deque (double-ended queue) is a dynamic data structure in C++ that allows elements to be added or removed from both the front and the rear. To use deque in your code, you need to include the header file .

2. Write a code snippet to create a deque of integers named intDeque.
3. How do you add elements to the front and back of a deque?

Answer: You can use the member functions

push_front()

and

push_back()

to add elements to the front and back of a deque, respectively.

4. Write a code snippet to add the numbers 1, 2, and 3 to the front of the deque
   intDeque
   .

5. How do you remove elements from the front and back of a deque?

Answer: You can use the member functions pop_front() and pop_back() to remove elements from the front and back of a deque, respectively.

6. Write a code snippet to remove the first and last elements of the deque
   intDeque
   .

7. How do you access the front and back elements of a deque without removing them?

Answer: You can use the member functions

front()

and

back()

to access the front and back elements of a deque without removing them.

8. Write a code snippet that prints the front and back elements of the deque
    intDeque

    .

9. How can you use a deque to implement a stack? Provide an example of pushing an element onto the stack and popping an element from the stack.

Answer: To implement a stack using a deque, you can use the

push_back()

and

pop_back()

functions to push and pop elements, respectively.

10. How can you use a deque to implement a queue? Provide an example of enqueuing an element and dequeuing an element.

Answer: To implement a queue using a deque, you can use the

push_back()

function to enqueue elements and the

pop_front()

function to dequeue elements.

C++ Graphs: The Web of Wonders Unraveled!

Greetings, fellow code wizards! Prepare to embark on a marvelous journey through the mystifying world of C++ Graphs—a land of wonder, intrigue, and the intricate web of interconnectedness. Prepare to delve into the labyrinthine realm of nodes, edges, adjacency lists, and adjacency matrices. Embrace your inner geek, summon your professional prowess, and clutch your sense of humor tightly as we unravel the enigma of C++ Graphs!

Graph Essentials

In the hallowed halls of Graph Theory, a graph is a collection of vertices (nodes) connected by edges (arcs). These enigmatic entities can manifest in various forms: directed or undirected, weighted or unweighted, cyclic or acyclic. Fear not, for we shall illuminate the path through this tangled maze of possibilities!

Graph Vertex and Edges: The Building Blocks of Connectivity

Greetings, fellow graph enthusiasts! Today, we'll dive into the exciting world of vertices and edges - the dynamic duo that forms the backbone of all graphs. But worry not, we'll keep it light and fun, because who doesn't love a bit of geeky humor?

First, let's talk about vertices (or nodes, if you prefer). In the graph universe, vertices are like the cool kids at school - they're the individual elements that make up a graph, each with their own unique identity. Imagine them as party guests, each bringing their own flair to the mix. And as you know, no party is complete without connections, right?

Enter the mighty edges, the lifeblood of any graph. These bad boys connect the vertices together, creating relationships between them. Just like friendships, edges can be one-way (directed) or two-way (undirected). So, whether you're a vertex looking for a casual acquaintance or a lifelong BFF, edges have got your back.

Now, you might be wondering, "How do vertices and edges come together to form a graph?" Well, think of a graph as a social network. Vertices are the people, and edges are the connections between them. The more connections there are, the richer and more complex the network becomes.

So, there you have it! Vertices and edges are the essential building blocks of any graph, forming a web of connections that can be as simple or as intricate as you like. Keep this dynamic duo in mind as we explore the fascinating world of graph theory, where vertices and edges take center stage in a dance of mathematical elegance. Stay tuned, and may the graph be with you!

Hello, graph aficionados! Today, we're going to explore the concept of neighbors in the vast and intriguing world of graphs. Don't worry, we'll keep it fun and geeky, because nothing says 'good time' quite like a healthy dose of graph-related humor!

In the graph realm, neighbors are like the friends next door - they're the vertices directly connected to each other by an edge. Think of a vertex as a person living in a house, and its neighbors as the folks in the adjacent houses. Whether it's borrowing a cup of sugar or simply waving hello, neighbors are there to make life a little more interesting.

Now, let's get down to the nitty-gritty of graph neighbors. When talking about neighbors, we usually refer to the vertices that share an edge with a given vertex. These vertices are considered "adjacent" to the vertex in question. For example, if vertex A is connected to vertex B by an edge, then A and B are neighbors, living side by side in perfect graph harmony.

But wait, there's more! Neighbors can also be classified according to the type of edge that connects them. For directed graphs, if there's an edge from vertex A to vertex B, then B is considered an "out-neighbor" of A, and A is an "in-neighbor" of B. In undirected graphs, the distinction between in-neighbors and out-neighbors doesn't exist, as the connection goes both ways, just like the love between true friends.

So, there you have it - neighbors are the vertices that share a connection in the exciting world of graphs. Whether it's a directed or undirected graph, neighbors make all the difference, creating rich and varied patterns of interaction. So, keep your friends close, and your graph neighbors closer, as we delve deeper into the fascinating universe of graph theory. Stay connected, and may the graph be with you!

Graph Degrees: A Measure of Popularity in the Graph Party

Greetings, graph enthusiasts! Are you ready for another journey into the wild and wonderful world of graph theory? Today, we're going to talk about graph degrees - a fascinating measure of a vertex's popularity at the ever-entertaining graph party. So, buckle up, and let's dive into the fun-filled realm of degrees, with a dash of humor and a side of geekiness!

In the graph universe, a degree is like a vertex's social standing - it tells us how many connections a vertex has with its neighbors. The higher the degree, the more popular the vertex is, and the more happening its social life! You could say that vertices with high degrees are the life of the graph party, while those with low degrees might be a bit more introverted.

Now, let's get a bit technical. The degree of a vertex is simply the number of edges incident to it, or in other words, the number of neighbors it has. In an undirected graph, calculating the degree is a breeze - just count the number of edges connected to the vertex. Easy peasy, lemon squeezy!

But wait, what about directed graphs? Fear not, graph fanatics, for we've got you covered! In directed graphs, we distinguish between "in-degree" and "out-degree". The in-degree of a vertex is the number of incoming edges (those directed towards the vertex), while the out-degree is the number of outgoing edges (those directed away from the vertex). Think of it like the number of people coming to a vertex's party versus those leaving. In-degree says, "Welcome, friends!" and out-degree says, "Goodbye, see you next time!"

So, there you have it - graph degrees, the measure of a vertex's popularity and connections in the exhilarating world of graphs. Whether you're dealing with directed or undirected graphs, remember that degrees are the key to understanding the intricate dance of vertex relationships. Stay tuned for more graph-tastic adventures, and always remember to party on, graph style!

Graph Paths: The Road Less Traveled in the Land of Graphs

Greetings, fellow graph enthusiasts! It's time to embark on another thrilling escapade through the whimsical world of graphs. In today's episode, we'll venture into the mysterious realm of graph paths - those serpentine trails that link vertices together in ways that would make even the most intrepid explorer's heart race. So grab your graph passport, buckle up, and let's hit the road with a geeky grin and a chuckle or two!

In the graph kingdom, paths are like the road trips of vertices - they connect our humble vertices together, traversing the breathtaking landscape of edges along the way. A path is a sequence of vertices, where each pair of consecutive vertices is connected by an edge. Sounds simple, right? But hold onto your hats, because the world of graph paths is as diverse and fascinating as the vertices they connect!

Paths can be short and sweet, like a quick jaunt to the corner store, or they can be long and winding, like a cross-country expedition. They can be simple, meaning they don't pass through the same vertex twice, or they can be more complex and circuitous, taking you on a tour of the same vertex multiple times. But fear not, intrepid pathfinders, for every path, no matter its twists and turns, has a purpose!

In graph theory, paths play a starring role in numerous algorithms and problem-solving techniques. From the shortest path problem, where we seek the most efficient route between two vertices, to the traveling salesperson problem, where we aim to visit all vertices in the graph with the least possible cost, paths are the bread and butter of graph exploration.

So, my fellow graph aficionados, we've reached the end of today's journey through the land of graph paths. Remember that paths are the lifeblood of graph exploration, connecting vertices in ways that can lead to the most unexpected and delightful of discoveries. Keep on exploring, charting new courses in the vast and wondrous world of graphs, and always remember to enjoy the journey with a side of geeky humor!

Graph Cycles: The Roller Coasters of the Graph World

Greetings once again, my graph-loving compatriots! Today, we shall embark on a thrilling, loop-de-loop adventure through the exhilarating world of graph cycles. Buckle up, hold on to your hats, and let's spin through this twisty-turny topic with all the geeky zeal and humor we can muster!

In the graph kingdom, cycles are the roller coasters of our delightful domain, bringing excitement and intrigue to our otherwise orderly landscapes. A cycle is a special kind of path, one that starts and ends at the same vertex, without visiting any other vertex more than once. These closed loops weave their way through the graph, traversing edges with the grace and gusto of an acrobat soaring through the air.

Cycles come in all shapes and sizes, from the petite and perfect triangles to the lengthy and labyrinthine, each with its own charm and allure. Some graphs are chock-full of cycles, creating intricate webs of vertices and edges that resemble the most elaborate of amusement park rides. Others may be more sparse, with only a smattering of cycles to offer a hint of excitement.

Much like their amusement park counterparts, cycles play a vital role in graph theory, making appearances in a wide array of algorithms and problems. From the famous Hamiltonian cycle problem, where we seek a cycle that visits all vertices exactly once, to the undeniably cool world of graph colorings, cycles are at the heart of some of the most captivating challenges in graph theory.

And with that, dear friends, our whirlwind tour of graph cycles comes to a close. As you continue your journey through the mesmerizing world of graphs, never forget the joy and intrigue that cycles bring to our beloved domain. Embrace the twists and turns, explore the ups and downs, and always remember to approach each new discovery with a geeky grin and a hearty chuckle!

Graph Connected Components: The Social Circles of Graph Land

Greetings, fellow graph enthusiasts and coding comrades! Today, we shall embark on a delightful journey into the realm of graph connected components, the social circles of our whimsical world of vertices and edges. As we venture forth, let's keep our geeky spirits high and our humor meters cranked up to the max!

In the magnificent land of graphs, connected components are like bustling social groups, where each vertex is a vibrant character connected to its friends through a dazzling network of edges. A connected component is a subgraph in which every vertex can reach every other vertex in the subgraph through a sequence of edges, while remaining completely separate from the other components. In simpler terms, connected components are like the cliques of Graph High School, where everyone in a group knows everyone else, but they might not be friends with those from other groups.

Just as every social circle has its unique charm and quirks, connected components come in various shapes and sizes, each boasting its own distinctive features. Some graphs may have a single, all-encompassing connected component that unites every vertex in harmonious togetherness, while others might be split into numerous smaller components, each merrily going about its own business.

The concept of connected components is crucial in numerous graph algorithms and problems, from the charmingly named "Friendship Circles" problem, where we seek the largest connected component in a social network, to the fascinating realm of minimum spanning trees, which strive to connect every vertex in a weighted graph with the least possible total weight.

As we conclude our delightful dive into graph connected components, remember to cherish the friendships and connections that make our graph world so vibrant and lively. Whether you're traversing the edges of a bustling social network or exploring the remote corners of a disconnected graph, always approach each new adventure with a geeky grin, a hearty laugh, and a keen sense of curiosity!

Types of the Graphs

Graph Battles: Directed vs. Undirected - Choose Your Champion!

Hear ye, hear ye, noble code knights and programming wizards! The time has come to witness an epic battle in the realm of Graph-landia: the mighty Directed Graph versus the valiant Undirected Graph! In this legendary clash of graph titans, we shall explore the distinguishing characteristics of these formidable foes and learn how to harness their powers for our coding quests. So, buckle up and prepare to be dazzled by the thrilling tale of Directed and Undirected Graphs!

In one corner, we have the fearsome Directed Graph, also known as the DiGraph. This mighty beast boasts edges with a sense of direction - from one vertex to another, but not the other way around! These arrows of destiny create a world of order and hierarchy, where vertices are bound by the chains of one-way relationships.

In the other corner, the noble Undirected Graph stands tall and proud. In this land of harmony and balance, edges form bidirectional connections between vertices. Here, relationships are mutual, and every path has a return journey, creating an intricate web of interdependence.

As you embark on your coding adventures through Graph-landia, you'll need to choose your champion wisely! The Directed Graph, with its strict order and hierarchy, excels in problems like dependency management, task scheduling, and modeling one-way relationships. On the other hand, the Undirected Graph, with its harmonious network of mutual connections, is a formidable ally in problems like social network analysis, pathfinding, and exploring symmetrical relationships.

So, brace yourselves, fellow code crusaders, and be prepared to face the challenges of Graph-landia with the help of your graph champions! With their unique powers and a hearty dose of humor, you'll conquer the coding battlegrounds with ease and grace. Onward, to victory and glory!

*A Tale of Two Graphs: The Weighted Wonders vs. the
Unweighted Underdogs*

Hark, fellow code wranglers and algorithm
aficionados! A new battle is brewing in the mystical
realm of Graph-landia: the epic showdown between
Weighted Wonders and Unweighted Underdogs! As
the tension mounts and the suspense builds, we shall
explore the unique features of these two graph
gladiators and how they can be harnessed to achieve
programming prowess. So, grab your popcorn and
settle in for a thrilling tale of weighty matters and
unburdened edges!

In the land of Weighted Wonders, each edge proudly
carries the burden of a numerical value, known as the
"weight." This weight can symbolize various
attributes, such as distances, costs, or capacities. In
this realm, the vertices are connected not only by
edges but also by the shared responsibility of
maintaining these values.

Meanwhile, in the domain of Unweighted Underdogs,
the edges remain blissfully unencumbered by
numerical values. These carefree connectors focus
solely on the relationships between vertices without
the added complexities of weights. While some might
call them lightweight, they offer simplicity and
elegance in their streamlined approach.

As you navigate the treacherous terrains of Graph-
landia, you must choose your graph champion wisely!
The Weighted Wonders, with their burdened edges

and versatile values, shine in problems involving shortest paths, minimum spanning trees, and network flows. In contrast, the Unweighted Underdogs, with their simple, unadorned connections, excel in problems like graph traversal, connectivity, and bipartite checking.

So, prepare to embark on a whirlwind adventure through the realms of Weighted Wonders and Unweighted Underdogs! With their distinct strengths and a dash of humor, you'll conquer the coding challenges that await you in the magical world of Graph-landia. Onward, to triumph and hilarity!

Graph Representations

Behold, the three primary representations of graphs in C++: Adjacency Matrices, List of Edges and Adjacency Lists.

Adjacency Matrices: Unraveling the Graph's Web of Connections

Greetings, fellow code sorcerers! Gather 'round as we embark on a new journey through the enchanting land of Graph Kingdom. Today, we shall unveil the arcane secrets of adjacency matrices - the formidable fortress that guards the graph's web of connections. So, ready your coding wands and join us in unearthing the mysteries of this powerful data structure!

Imagine, if you will, a great mapmaker charting the Graph Kingdom. Instead of recording each vertex's connections in a list, they create a grand matrix that captures the entire realm's connections. The mapmaker's masterpiece, dear coders, is none other than the adjacency matrix.

An adjacency matrix is a square matrix that represents a graph, with rows and columns representing vertices, and each cell containing a value that indicates the presence or absence of an edge between the corresponding vertices. With its rigid structure and efficient space utilization, the adjacency matrix is perfect for dense graphs or when fast edge queries are vital.

To summon the power of adjacency matrices, we shall weave our C++ incantations:

Behold the majesty of the adjacency matrix! In just a few lines of code, we've conjured a graph representation that offers blazing-fast edge queries and the ability to store edge weights or properties. Whether your quest leads you to the bustling cities of Graph Kingdom or the quiet, interconnected villages, adjacency matrices will steadfastly guide your way.

So, brave code wizards, venture forth armed with your newfound knowledge and conquer the Graph Kingdom with the mighty power of adjacency matrices! May your matrices be ever efficient, your coding challenges met with confidence, and your adventures filled with fun and excitement!

Greetings, code-wielding compatriots! Today, we embark on a grand adventure to the realm of Graph Kingdom, where vertices and edges reign supreme. In this mystical land, we shall explore the concept of adjacency lists – the little black book of graph relationships. So, strap on your coding boots, and let's unravel the enigmatic secrets of this ingenious data structure!

Now, imagine, if you will, a grand ball at the Graph Kingdom palace. Vertices dance and mingle, their edges intertwined in a dizzying waltz of connections. Amidst the revelry, a trusty scribe (that's you!) diligently records each vertex's dance partners in a tome known as the adjacency list.

An adjacency list, dear coders, is a clever way of representing a graph, where each vertex holds a list of its neighboring vertices. It elegantly captures the connections between vertices, allowing for efficient traversal and queries. So, how does one create this magical data structure, you ask? Fear not, for we shall delve into the depths of code, weaving spells of C++ to bring our adjacency list to life:

Behold the beauty of the adjacency list! With just a few lines of code, we've conjured a graph representation that's easy to understand and efficient to traverse. Whether your quest takes you to the realm of social networks, mapping the world, or finding the shortest path to the nearest pub, adjacency lists will guide you on your journey.

So, code wizards, venture forth with your newfound knowledge and wield the power of adjacency lists to conquer the Graph Kingdom! May your traversals be swift, your queries snappy, and your coding adventures filled with joy and wonder!

List of Edges: The Lightweight Graph Traveler's Essential Tool

Ahoy, noble code adventurers! As we continue to traverse the mystical lands of Graph Kingdom, it's time to pack your bags with another versatile tool - the list of edges. This lightweight and handy contraption will assist you in navigating the graph's connections with ease and speed. So, gather 'round, and let us unravel the secrets of this wondrous data structure, using the language of C++ and a hearty dose of humor.

Picture yourself as a swift and agile graph traveler, eager to explore every nook and cranny of the Graph Kingdom. Instead of lugging around the heavy baggage of adjacency matrices or the cumbersome scrolls of adjacency lists, you opt for a simple, yet effective, list of edges. This humble collection captures the essence of the graph's connections without any unnecessary frills, making it perfect for sparse graphs or algorithms that require an edge-centric approach.

To harness the power of the list of edges, we must first craft our C++ incantation:

Behold the elegance of the list of edges! With this magical incantation, you've conjured a graph representation that's lightweight and edge-focused. No more heavy matrices or bulky lists to slow you down on your journey through the Graph Kingdom.

Remember, brave code explorers, while the list of edges might not be as feature-rich as its bulkier cousins, it's an invaluable tool for those who prefer a minimalist approach. So, stride forth into the Graph Kingdom, armed with the list of edges, and conquer the coding challenges that await you. May your travels be filled with laughter, learning, and the satisfaction of a well-crafted algorithm!

Graph Alchemy: Turning Lists of Edges into Adjacency Lists

Greetings, valiant code warriors! As you venture into the realm of coding challenges, you'll often stumble upon graph problems that provide the input as a list of edges. Fear not! For today, we shall unlock the mystical art of graph alchemy and transform these lists of edges into adjacency lists, using the enchanted incantations of C++ and a sprinkle of humor.

In the Graph Kingdom, every coding hero should master the art of adaptation. When confronted with a list of edges, use your newfound skills to transmute them into adjacency lists, thus revealing the hidden connections within. Behold the arcane formula:

By the power of graph alchemy, you've now transformed the list of edges into a shimmering adjacency list, unveiling the hidden structure of the Graph Kingdom. This potent transmutation will empower you to tackle even the most daunting graph challenges with ease and finesse.

So, charge forth, noble code crusaders, and wield the power of graph alchemy to conquer the coding challenges that lie ahead. With a dash of wit and a hearty laugh, may your journey through the Graph Kingdom be filled with triumph and delight!

Graph Traversal: A Whimsical Wander Through Vertex Village

Greetings, graph gurus and coding conquerors! Today, we'll embark on a whimsical wander through Vertex Village, exploring the wonderful world of graph traversal. So, strap on your virtual hiking boots and grab your coding compass, as we set out on a delightful journey filled with geeky giggles and algorithmic antics!

Graph traversal is the captivating process of visiting each vertex in a graph while following its edges, much like a cheerful stroll through Vertex Village's charming streets and winding alleyways. This thrilling voyage can lead to the discovery of hidden treasures, secret pathways, and the joyful bonds that connect the inhabitants of our graphy kingdom. There are two major traversal techniques that intrepid explorers like yourself can employ: Depth-First Search (DFS) and Breadth-First Search (BFS).

DFS is akin to a daring spelunker delving deep into the twisting tunnels of a graph, exploring each path as far as possible before backtracking to uncover new routes. It's an adventurous and bold approach that uses a stack (or recursion, for those daring enough) to guide its courageous course.

BFS, on the other hand, is like a leisurely stroll through the park, visiting each vertex layer by layer in a more methodical fashion. It relies on a trusty queue to navigate its way, ensuring that it never strays too far from its starting point before venturing onward to new horizons.

Both DFS and BFS have their unique charms and strengths, and each can be employed to solve a multitude of problems in the enchanting realm of graphs. Whether you're searching for the shortest path between two vertices, identifying connected components, or simply taking in the picturesque scenery of Vertex Village, these traversal techniques are your trusty guides on this exciting expedition.

As we wrap up our delightful foray into graph traversal, remember that no matter which path you choose – be it the deep, daring dives of DFS or the breezy, systematic strolls of BFS – always tackle your graph quests with a geeky grin, a hearty chuckle, and a zest for coding adventure!

Breadth-First Search: A Leisurely Jaunt Through Vertex Village

Greetings, coding comrades! Today, we embark on a leisurely jaunt through the delightful neighborhood of Vertex Village, guided by the ever-reliable Breadth-First Search (BFS). We'll amble along the edges, popping in on vertices like friendly neighbors while we traverse the graph. So, dust off your favorite queue and let's dive into the mirthful meanderings of BFS!

The heart of BFS is a trusty queue, which helps us keep track of the vertices we've visited and the order in which we visit them. Let's take a look at an example in C++:

Let's take a whimsical walk through this code, shall we? We begin by initializing our visited vector, ensuring that each vertex starts with a "haven't met the neighbors" status. Next, we create our trusty queue and add our starting vertex, marking it as visited in the process.

Now, the BFS dance begins! While our queue is not empty, we dequeue the first vertex in line (let's call it the "host" vertex), and pay it a visit. This is our chance to catch up on the latest gossip and admire the vertex's garden. Once we've had our fill of pleasantries, we loop through the host vertex's neighbors, checking if we've visited them before. If not, we mark them as visited and add them to our queue for future exploration.

As we repeat this process, we ensure that we visit each vertex at a safe and leisurely pace, moving through the graph layer by layer. When our queue is finally empty, we've successfully visited every vertex in Vertex Village, and our BFS journey comes to a delightful close.

There you have it, folks! BFS, the friendly and systematic guide to traversing graphs, always ready to accompany you on a jovial jaunt through Vertex Village. With a geeky grin and a hearty chuckle, you'll be traversing graphs like a seasoned BFS explorer in no time!

Recursive BFS: Unraveling the Mysteries of Vertex Village with a Twist

Greetings once more, my programming pals! It's time to embark on yet another adventurous journey through the enchanting Vertex Village, but this time, we're spicing things up a bit. That's right, we're tackling the mystical, and slightly rebellious, world of recursive Breadth-First Search (BFS)! So, brace yourselves for an exciting expedition, packed with laughter, wonder, and recursion!

Before we begin, let's address the recursive elephant in the room: Recursive BFS is less common than its iterative counterpart, mainly due to its increased complexity and the risk of running into stack overflow issues. However, the spirit of geeky exploration compels us to attempt this unorthodox approach, just for the sheer joy of it! Now, without further ado, let's unveil the code:

In this code, we have separated the core BFS logic into a

recursive_bfs

function that takes a queue, a visited vector, and an adjacency list as its arguments. The base case is when our queue is empty, signifying that we have traversed the entire graph.

Now, let's traverse this recursive rollercoaster together! The process begins in a similar fashion to iterative BFS. We visit the "host" vertex, dequeue it, and then explore its neighbors. The magic happens when we call

recursive_bfs

at the end of the function, effectively looping through our BFS algorithm in a recursive manner.

As for the comparison between iterative and recursive BFS, the recursive approach may appear more elegant to some, but it's not without its risks. With a deeper graph, recursion can lead to stack overflow issues, causing your program to crash and burn (metaphorically speaking). The iterative BFS, on the other hand, is often safer and more efficient.

However, as explorers of the geeky realm, we must venture into the depths of recursion, even if just for the thrill of it!

In conclusion, recursive BFS is a wild and whimsical ride through Vertex Village, filled with excitement, challenges, and perhaps even a touch of danger. So, tread carefully, my fellow geeks, and always remember to laugh in the face of stack overflow!

DFS: Delving into the Mysterious Maze of Graph Grotto

Greetings, my fellow code aficionados! Get ready for a thrilling expedition into the enigmatic depths of Graph Grotto as we dive into the world of Depth-First Search (DFS)! Sharpen your wits, grab your coding gear, and let's embark on a journey filled with geeky excitement, witty humor, and, of course, DFS!

DFS is like navigating a complex maze, taking every path to the end before backtracking and exploring other routes. It's an adventurous and daring algorithm that isn't afraid to get lost in the depths of Graph Grotto. Now, let's unravel the mysteries of DFS through the magical language of C++:

Let's dive deep into the code together, exploring every twist and turn of this marvelous maze! Our magical journey begins with the dfs function, which takes a vertex, a visited vector, and an adjacency list as its trusty companions.

As we step into Graph Grotto, we mark our current vertex as visited and proudly announce our arrival with a cheerful cout statement. Then, we venture forth into the dark corners of the grotto by exploring each unvisited neighbor, recursively invoking the dfs function and plunging deeper into the depths of Graph Grotto.

Once we've reached the end of a path, our trusty recursion will guide us back to the previous junction, allowing us to explore other routes in our quest to uncover the secrets of the grotto.

In conclusion, DFS is a daring and adventurous algorithm that's not afraid to delve deep into the unknown realms of Graph Grotto. As intrepid explorers of the coding world, we must embrace the thrill of the unknown and boldly venture forth into the enigmatic depths of DFS. So, my geeky compatriots, let's raise our coding torches high and conquer the mysterious maze of Graph Grotto!

Iterative DFS: The Unconventional Pathfinder of the Graph Jungle

Greetings, coding comrades! It's time to step into the vibrant and tangled realm of the Graph Jungle, where we'll meet the unconventional and daring pathfinder: the Iterative Depth-First Search (DFS)! Prepare for a wild ride filled with geeky delight, witty repartee, and the ever-captivating Iterative DFS!

While the Recursive DFS is a true maze-master, the Iterative DFS has its own unique charm, conquering the Graph Jungle with a stack and an undaunted spirit. So, grab your coding machetes and let's explore the untamed world of Iterative DFS in C++:

Hold on to your coding hats, fellow geeks, as we embark on an exhilarating journey through the Iterative DFS code! Our adventure begins with the

iterative_dfs

function, accompanied by our trusty allies: the start vertex, adjacency list, visited vector, and our ever-faithful stack,

s

.

With our initial vertex in hand, we boldly push it onto the stack and mark it as visited. Then, we venture into the wilds of the Graph Jungle, hacking our way through its dense undergrowth with our trusty

while

loop.

As we traverse the jungle, we pop the top vertex from the stack, proudly announcing our presence at each new vertex with a triumphant cout statement. We then explore the neighboring vertices, pushing the unvisited ones onto our stack and marking them as visited, navigating the depths of the Graph Jungle one vertex at a time.

The Iterative DFS is the unconventional pathfinder of the Graph Jungle, fearlessly exploring its tangled depths with a stack and an unyielding spirit. So, my fellow code warriors, let's join forces with this daring algorithm and conquer the wilds of the Graph Jungle! Onward, to coding glory!

Ladies and gentlemen, code enthusiasts and geeky gladiators, gather 'round! Today, we present to you the ultimate showdown: the BFS and DFS Battle Royale, where we explore the various versions of these valiant graph traversing warriors!

In one corner, we have the courageous and quick-witted Breadth-First Search (BFS), navigating the Graph Jungle with its trusty queue, expanding outwards from the starting vertex. And in the other corner, we have the daring and deep-diving Depth-First Search (DFS), boldly traversing the deepest recesses of the Graph Jungle with its trusty stack or fearless recursion.

These champions of code come in various flavors, each with its own unique appeal:

1. Iterative BFS: The Iterative BFS thrives on a steady diet of loops and queues, exploring the Graph Jungle layer by layer. With its trusty queue, this BFS variant moves outwards from

the starting vertex, visiting each neighbor before venturing deeper into the jungle.

2. Recursive BFS: While less common, the Recursive BFS is a rare and exotic breed, using recursion to achieve its breadth-first traversal. This version employs a creative and recursive approach to visit neighboring vertices before exploring deeper layers of the Graph Jungle.

3. Recursive DFS: The Recursive DFS is the epitome of elegance and simplicity, diving deep into the Graph Jungle with a fearless spirit of recursion. This version takes a plunge into the depths, visiting each vertex along a path before backtracking and exploring alternative paths.

4. Iterative DFS: The Iterative DFS is the unconventional pathfinder, armed with a trusty stack, conquering the Graph Jungle by visiting vertices one at a time. With a spirit of adventure, this DFS variant uses a loop and stack to dive deep, popping vertices off the stack to explore new paths.

As the BFS and DFS gladiators battle it out in the Graph Jungle, each champion showcases its own unique talents and techniques. Whether you favor the swift and expansive BFS, or the bold and deep-diving DFS, these versatile warriors of code will surely leave you in awe.

So, fellow geeks, choose your champion and join the BFS & DFS showdown! May the best algorithm prevail!

Summary

It's grass-planting season on Farmer John's farm, which consists of N fields (1 <= N <= 105), conveniently numbered 1...N and connected by N-1 bidirectional pathways. Each field can be reached from any other field via these pathways.

Farmer John wants to minimize the number of grass types he plants, as more variety means higher expenses. However, his cows have become quite particular about their grass selections. They'll complain if the same type of grass is found in adjacent fields or even nearly-adjacent fields (both directly connected to a common field).

To avoid grumpy cows and their mischief, help Farmer John find the minimum number of grass types he needs for his farm, keeping the cows' picky preferences in mind. Let's balance their refined tastes with Farmer John's expenses and find the most cost-effective solution to this grassy conundrum!

Analyze

Let's embark on this grassy adventure and dive into Farmer John's conundrum! We'll analyze the problem and devise an approach to ensure his cows' sophisticated palates are satisfied, while also minimizing the cost of grass types.

As we examine the problem, we'll notice that the farm's field connectivity resembles a tree structure. In this tree, each node represents a field, and the edges represent the pathways between them. To satisfy the cows' refined tastes, we'll need to avoid using the same grass type in adjacent or nearly-adjacent fields. That's where the magic happens!

One approach to this problem is to use a graph-coloring algorithm. Since we want to minimize the number of grass types, we'll aim for the lowest possible chromatic number. It turns out that our tree-like structure saves the day - for a tree graph, the chromatic number is always 2. This means we only need two types of grass to keep the cows content!

We can implement this solution using a depth-first search (DFS) algorithm or a breadth-first search (BFS) algorithm. Traverse the graph while alternating between grass types as we move from one field to another. By doing so, we ensure no two adjacent or nearly-adjacent fields have the same grass type.

So, there you have it! A brilliant blend of graph theory and bovine satisfaction to solve this problem with a touch of geeky humor. In the end, Farmer John can simply use two types of grass, saving his wallet and keeping his cows from turning into grass connoisseurs!

Exercises: C++ Graphs: The Web of Wonders Unraveled!

1. What is a graph data structure, and what are its main components?

Answer: A graph is a data structure consisting of a finite set of vertices (or nodes) and a finite set of edges connecting the vertices. The main components of a graph are vertices and edges.

2. What is the difference between a directed and an undirected graph?

Answer: In a directed graph, each edge has an initial vertex (tail) and a terminal vertex (head), indicating a one-way relationship between vertices. In an undirected graph, edges do not have an initial or terminal vertex, indicating a two-way relationship between vertices.

3. Name two common ways to represent a graph in C++.

Answer: Two common ways to represent a graph in C++ are adjacency matrix and adjacency list.

4. Write a code snippet to represent an undirected graph using an adjacency list in C++.

5. What is the time complexity of searching for an edge in an adjacency matrix and an adjacency list?

Answer: The time complexity of searching for an edge in an adjacency matrix is O(1), while in an adjacency list, it is O(V) for an undirected graph and O(E) for a directed graph.

6. What is a weighted graph?

Answer: A weighted graph is a graph in which each edge has an associated weight or cost. The weights can represent distances, costs, capacities, etc.

7. Explain the difference between depth-first search (DFS) and breadth-first search (BFS) algorithms.

Answer: Depth-first search (DFS) is a graph traversal algorithm that explores as far as possible along a branch before backtracking. It can be implemented using recursion or an explicit stack. Breadth-first search (BFS) is a graph traversal algorithm that explores all vertices at the current level before moving on to vertices at the next level. It is implemented using a queue.

8. Write a code snippet to perform a DFS traversal on an undirected graph using recursion.

9. What are some common graph algorithms?

Answer: Some common graph algorithms are depth-first search (DFS), breadth-first search (BFS), Dijkstra's shortest path algorithm, Bellman-Ford algorithm, Kruskal's minimum spanning tree algorithm, Prim's minimum spanning tree algorithm, and Floyd-Warshall algorithm.

10. Explain how you would detect a cycle in an undirected graph using DFS.

Answer: To detect a cycle in an undirected graph using DFS, start a DFS traversal from every unvisited node. During the traversal, if you encounter a node that has been visited and is not the parent of the current node, then there is a cycle in the graph.

Algorithms: The Magic Behind Computing

Greetings, fellow enthusiasts of the arcane arts of computing! It is our great honor to welcome you to the enchanting realm of algorithms—a place where logic, creativity, and computational prowess collide to create the magic that drives our digital world. With an open mind and an insatiable curiosity, prepare to embark on a captivating journey through the wondrous world of algorithms!

Algorithms, the mystical incantations at the heart of every computational endeavor, are step-by-step procedures for solving problems, carrying out tasks, or performing calculations. Like masterful sorcerers, they harness the power of logic to transform raw data into valuable insights, magnificent solutions, and awe-inspiring feats of digital wizardry. From the humblest of sorting tasks to the grandest of artificial intelligence ventures, algorithms stand as the foundation upon which our digital empires are built.

In the vast expanse of the algorithmic universe, we find a myriad of magical creatures, each with its unique talents and purpose. There are the Sorting Algorithms, noble guardians of order in the digital realm, who bring harmony to unordered data. The Search Algorithms, intrepid explorers of information, tirelessly seek the answers to our most pressing questions. And let us not forget the Graph Algorithms, architects of interconnectedness, who deftly navigate the labyrinthine networks that bind our world together.

As we delve deeper into the arcane world of algorithms, we must be mindful of their power and respect the delicate balance between complexity and efficiency. For in this enchanted land, time and space are precious commodities, and it is the responsibility of every algorithmic sorcerer to wield their powers with care and precision.

With an unquenchable thirst for knowledge and a passion for the art of problem-solving, you are now prepared to embark on a grand adventure through the mesmerizing world of algorithms. Embrace the challenges, revel in the victories, and celebrate the sheer magic that awaits you in this realm of limitless possibilities.

Now, go forth and conquer, noble champions of the algorithmic arts!

A Tale of Two Complexities: Runtime and Space in the Algorithmic Kingdom

Greetings, intrepid explorers of the algorithmic realm! Today, we embark upon a thrilling journey through the mystical lands of runtime and space complexity—the twin forces governing the delicate balance of power in our enchanting world of algorithms. So, strap on your thinking caps, channel your inner computational wizard, and let's dive headfirst into the spellbinding world of complexity!

In the grand kingdom of algorithms, the magical spells that bring order to the digital realm, performance is of paramount importance. For it is not enough to conjure a solution; one must also do so with grace, efficiency, and a flair for the dramatic. Enter our valiant heroes, runtime complexity and space complexity—the noble guardians of algorithmic performance.

Runtime complexity, the swifter of the two, holds dominion over the passage of time. As the algorithms weave their intricate spells, runtime complexity measures the speed and efficiency of their incantations. It is a powerful force, capable of turning the slowest, most cumbersome spells into blindingly fast feats of computational sorcery. But beware, dear traveler, for the swiftest solution is not always the best!

O(1) - Constant Time Complexity:

Constant time complexity refers to an algorithm that takes the same amount of time to execute, regardless of the input size. A classic example of O(1) complexity is accessing an element in an array by its index:

No matter how large the array is, the time it takes to access an element using its index remains the same.

O(n) - Linear Time Complexity:

Linear time complexity refers to an algorithm that takes time proportional to the input size. The time it takes to execute increases linearly as the input size grows. A typical example of $O(n)$ complexity is iterating through elements in an array:

In this example, the time it takes to execute the loop is proportional to the number of elements in the array.

O(n^2) - Quadratic Time Complexity:

Quadratic time complexity refers to an algorithm that takes time proportional to the square of the input size. The time it takes to execute increases quadratically as the input size grows. A classic example of $O(n^2)$ complexity is the nested loop, which is often used in naive sorting algorithms like Bubble Sort:

In this example, the outer loop iterates 'n' times, and for each iteration, the inner loop also iterates 'n' times, resulting in a total of n * n = n^2 iterations, hence the $O(n^2)$ complexity.

O(log(n)) - Logarithmic Time Complexity:

Logarithmic time complexity refers to an algorithm that reduces the input size by a constant factor with each step. A classic example of $O(\log(n))$ complexity is Binary Search:

In this example, the search space is reduced by half in each iteration, resulting in a logarithmic runtime complexity.

O(nlog(n)) - Linearithmic Time Complexity:

Linearithmic time complexity refers to an algorithm that takes time proportional to the input size times the logarithm of the input size. A classic example of O(nlog(n)) complexity is the Merge Sort algorithm:

n this example, the input is repeatedly divided into halves (log(n) divisions) and then combined in a linear fashion (n operations), resulting in a linearithmic runtime complexity.

O(2^n) - Exponential Time Complexity:

Exponential time complexity refers to an algorithm whose runtime doubles with each addition to the input size. A classic example of O(2^n) complexity is the recursive calculation of Fibonacci numbers:

In this example, the function calls itself twice for each non-base case input, resulting in an exponential growth of the number of function calls, and thus an exponential runtime complexity.

Space complexity, the more grounded of the pair, reigns over the realm of memory. It is the keeper of the keys, the master of the vaults, the protector of the precious resources that fuel our algorithmic spells. As we conjure solutions from the digital ether, space complexity ensures that our enchantments remain efficient, compact, and sustainable. For even in the vast expanse of the algorithmic kingdom, space is a precious commodity, not to be squandered on reckless incantations.

As we traverse the enchanting lands of runtime and space complexity, we must strive for balance and harmony in our algorithmic spells. For it is only through the delicate interplay of these twin forces that we can unlock the true potential of our computational prowess.

So, go forth, brave adventurers, and seek the wisdom of runtime and space complexity as you delve deeper into the mystical world of algorithms. May your incantations be swift, your spells efficient, and your journey through the enchanted realm of complexity filled with wonder, discovery, and perhaps a touch of whimsy.

Example: 2017 January Contest, Bronze Problem 1. Don't Be Last!

Summary

Farmer John's 7 dairy divas are Bessie, Elsie, Daisy, Gertie, Annabelle, Maggie, and Henrietta. Meticulously recording their milk production, Farmer John cherishes his high-yielding heifers.

Now, cows are no workaholics; they'd love nothing more than being the least productive moo-chine. But they've overheard Farmer John's "farm to table" conversations and have grown suspicious. Being the lowest producer might not be the wisest choice. So, they set their sights on the next best thing: producing the second-lowest amount of milk in the herd. Time to find the cow who currently reigns supreme in this sweet spot.

Let's help these cunning cows determine which one of them has achieved this comfortable yet safe position in the milking hierarchy. Hold on to your hooves; we're about to unveil the second-to-last milk mogul!

Analyze

To help our 7 dairy dames figure out which of them is comfortably producing the second-smallest amount of milk, we need to dive into the data. Farmer John's fastidious record-keeping comes in handy here, as we will examine each cow's milk production in detail.

We'll first gather the daily milk production numbers for each cow. The next step is to sort these quantities in ascending order. Be ready for some udderly delightful data wrangling!

With the milk production figures sorted, we can identify the second-lowest value on the list. This is the golden ticket, the sweet spot our bovine buddies are striving to achieve. By finding the cow who corresponds to this particular milk production value, we'll reveal the lucky lady who has managed to strike the perfect balance.

So, let's embark on this moovelous adventure and unearth the secret identity of the second-to-last milky mastermind!

Exercises: A Tale of Two Complexities: Runtime and Space in the Algorithmic Kingdom

1. What is time complexity in the context of algorithms?

Answer: Time complexity is the amount of time an algorithm takes to run as a function of the size of the input data. It provides an estimation of the performance of an algorithm, helping to compare different algorithms and determine which one is more efficient for a specific task.

2. What is space complexity in the context of algorithms?

Answer: Space complexity is the amount of memory an algorithm uses as a function of the size of the input data. It provides an estimation of the memory requirements of an algorithm, helping to compare different algorithms and determine which one is more memory-efficient for a specific task.

3. What is the Big O notation, and what does it represent?

Answer: Big O notation is a way to describe the performance of an algorithm by representing the upper bound of its growth rate. It shows the relationship between the size of the input data and the number of operations or memory usage, allowing for a comparison of different algorithms' efficiency.

4. What is the time complexity of the following code snippet?

Answer: The time complexity of this code snippet is O(n^2) because there are two nested loops, each running for 'n' iterations.

5. What is the space complexity of the following code snippet?

Answer: The space complexity of this code snippet is O(1) because the memory usage does not depend on the size of the input array. Only a single integer variable 'sum' is used, which occupies constant space.

6. What is the time complexity of the binary search algorithm?

Answer: The time complexity of the binary search algorithm is O(log n) because, in each iteration, the search space is reduced by half.

7. Write a code snippet for a function that has a time complexity of O(n) and space complexity of O(n).

8. How does the time complexity of the Quick Sort algorithm change in the worst-case, average-case, and best-case scenarios?

Answer: For the Quick Sort algorithm, the time complexity is O(n^2) in the worst-case scenario, O(n log n) in the average-case scenario, and O(n log n) in the best-case scenario.

9. What is the time complexity of the Merge Sort algorithm, and what is its space complexity?

Answer: The time complexity of the Merge Sort algorithm is O(n log n) in all scenarios (worst-case, average-case, and best-case). Its space complexity is O(n), as it requires additional memory for the merging process.

10. Explain the difference between constant time (O(1)), linear time (O(n)), and quadratic time (O(n^2)) complexities.

- Constant time (O(1)) complexity refers to an algorithm whose execution time remains constant regardless of the input size. Examples include array access, basic arithmetic operations, and simple statements.
- Linear time (O(n)) complexity refers to an algorithm whose execution time is directly proportional to the input size. As the input size increases, the time taken by the algorithm increases linearly. Examples include simple loops, searching for an element in an array, or summing the elements of an array.
- Quadratic time (O(n^2)) complexity refers to an algorithm whose execution time is proportional to the square of the input size. As the input size increases, the time taken by the algorithm increases quadratically. Examples include nested loops, bubble sort, and insertion sort.

In summary, constant time complexity represents algorithms with constant execution time, regardless of input size; linear time complexity represents algorithms whose execution time is proportional to the input size; and quadratic time complexity represents algorithms whose execution time is proportional to the square of the input size.

The Fabulous Four: Marvelous Min, Mighty Max, Astounding Avg, and Sensational Sum in C++

Hark, fair travelers of the coding realm! Gather 'round as we regale you with tales of the Fabulous Four – the legendary algorithms that have captivated programmers for generations. These magnificent heroes – Marvelous Min, Mighty Max, Astounding Avg, and Sensational Sum – wield the awesome power of C++ to perform their extraordinary feats of computational derring-do. So, without further ado, let's meet these awe-inspiring algorithms and learn the secrets of their enchanting ways.

Marvelous Min, the diminutive defender of the smallest values, leaps into action with lightning speed to find the tiniest element in an array or vector. With a flourish of C++ magic, the spellbinding

min_element

function from the

library empowers our pint-sized protagonist to save the day:

Mighty Max, the towering titan of the tallest values, fearlessly scales the heights of data structures in search of the greatest element. Unleashing the formidable power of the max_element

function from the

library, our valiant hero soars above the competition:

Astounding Avg, the mesmerizing maestro of the middle ground, weaves a symphony of numbers to compute the harmonic mean of an array or vector. With the help of Sensational Sum, our musical mastermind effortlessly orchestrates the perfect performance:

Sensational Sum, the extravagant entertainer of the algorithmic stage, dazzles audiences with a spectacular display of summation skills. Employing the awe-inspiring

accumulate

function from the

library, our captivating conjurer brings an array or vector's elements together in a grand finale:

And so, dear friends, our tale of the Fabulous Four comes to a close. Armed with the power of C++, these legendary algorithms have once again demonstrated their prowess in the ever-changing world of programming. May the wisdom of Marvelous Min, Mighty Max, Astounding Avg, and Sensational Sum guide you on your coding adventures, filling your journey with wonder, excitement, and a touch of algorithmic magic.

Example: 2015 December Contest, Bronze Problem 1. Fence Painting

Summary

After enduring several seasons of extreme temperatures, Farmer John decides it's time to repaint his fence with the assistance of his talented cow, Bessie. Although Bessie is surprisingly skilled at painting, she struggles to follow Farmer John's directions.

Visualizing the fence as a one-dimensional number line, Farmer John paints the section from x=a to x=b. For instance, when a=3 and b=5, he covers an interval of length 2. Bessie, misinterpreting his instructions, paints the segment from x=c to x=d, which may overlap with all or part of Farmer John's section. The task is to find the total length of the fence now coated with paint.

Analyze

In this section, we'll take a closer look at the fence painting problem, unravel its complexities, and lay a solid foundation for our solution. After all, as the great Sherlock Holmes once said, "It is a capital mistake to theorize before one has data." So, let's gather our thoughts and analyze the problem like true coding detectives!

The given problem presents us with Farmer John's and Bessie's painted fence sections, represented as intervals on a number line (x=a to x=b and x=c to x=d). Our task is to determine the total length of the fence covered in paint. To approach this problem, we must first observe the relationships between the two intervals. They can either overlap or be disjoint, and depending on this relationship, our method for calculating the total painted length will vary.

To make the problem more manageable, we can break it down into smaller subproblems. Firstly, we need to determine if the intervals overlap or not. Next, we calculate the lengths of the individual painted sections. If there's an overlap, we must also calculate the length of the overlapped segment. Finally, we can combine these calculated lengths to obtain the total painted length.

With a clear understanding of the problem and its subproblems, we can now identify suitable algorithms or approaches to tackle each of them. In this case, basic arithmetic operations, comparisons, and conditional statements can be used to address the subproblems and arrive at the solution.

As we craft our solution, it's important to consider any edge cases or potential pitfalls. For instance, we should ensure that our calculations handle cases where the intervals have zero overlap or when one interval is completely contained within the other. By carefully considering these edge cases, we can construct a robust and accurate solution to the problem at hand.

By thoroughly analyzing the fence painting problem, we have laid a strong foundation for solving it. With a clear understanding of the problem's structure and nuances, we are now better equipped to devise an efficient and accurate solution. So, let's roll up our sleeves and get coding!

Solution

Example: 2022 December Contest, Bronze Problem 1. Cow College

Summary

At Farmer John's Cow University, there are N ($1 <= N <= 105$) prospective students eager to learn. Each cow has a maximum tuition threshold of ci ($1 <= ci <= 106$) that they're willing to pay. Farmer John must decide on the tuition fee, which will apply to all cows.

If the tuition surpasses a cow's maximum limit, that cow will decide not to enroll. Farmer John's goal is to maximize his revenue to provide his instructors with a fair salary. The challenge is to figure out the optimum tuition fee and calculate the maximum amount of money he can make.

Let's embark on this academic adventure to find the perfect balance between milking the cows for all they're worth and maintaining a bovine-friendly budget. With our geeky, professional, and humorous approach, we're sure to identify the udderly perfect solution!

Analyze

Analyzing this problem requires us to find the ideal tuition that brings in the most revenue without alienating potential students. While it might be tempting to set the tuition fee sky-high, this would result in a lonely campus with only a few cows able to afford such astronomical costs. On the other hand, making it too affordable would lead to a packed university with not enough income to support the staff.

To tackle this conundrum, we can take a step-by-step approach that involves sorting the cows based on their maximum tuition thresholds. This allows us to calculate the potential revenue for each possible tuition fee, ultimately identifying the one that maximizes Farmer John's income.

First, we'll sort the cows by their maximum tuition thresholds in ascending order. Then, we'll iterate through the sorted list of cows, computing the potential revenue for each tuition value. We'll consider the number of cows who would attend the university at that tuition level, and multiply it by the tuition fee.

As we traverse the tuition possibilities, we'll keep track of the highest revenue and corresponding tuition value. Once we've analyzed all the options, we'll present the maximum revenue and the optimal tuition fee.

With our geeky, professional, and good-humored perspective, we'll not only help Farmer John find the perfect tuition for his Cow University but also keep the cow students from experiencing a financial squeeze. So let's get moooo-ving and find that sweet spot for Farmer John's academic empire!

Solution

Exercises: The Fabulous Four: Marvelous Min, Mighty Max, Astounding Avg, and Sensational Sum in C++

1. Write a C++ function that takes an array of integers and returns the maximum value in the array.
2. What is the output of the following code snippet?

Answer: The output will be

28

, as the code calculates the sum of the elements in the

numbers

array.

3. Write a C++ function that calculates the average of the elements in a vector of doubles.

Answer:

4. Given a vector of integers, write a C++ function that returns a pair containing the minimum and maximum values in the vector.
5. What is the time complexity of finding the minimum value in an array of integers?

Answer: The time complexity is O(n), where n is the number of elements in the array.

6. Write a C++ function that takes an array of integers and its size, then returns the index of the maximum value in the array.
7. Write a C++ function that calculates the sum of all even numbers in a given vector of integers.
8. What is the output of the following code snippet?

Answer: The output will be

120

, as the code calculates the product of the elements in the

numbers

vector.

9. Write a C++ function that calculates the average of all odd numbers in a given vector of integers.

Sorting Serenade: Harmonizing Arrays and Vectors with C++

Hear ye, hear ye, coding aficionados! A wondrous tale of algorithmic artistry awaits as we embark on a melodious journey through the realm of C++ sorting. Prepare to be regaled by the harmonious notes of ascending and descending elements, as we learn the enchanting secrets of transforming disarray into sweet symphony.

Behold the Sorting Serenade, a dazzling performance composed by the versatile maestro of the

library, the

sort()

function. With a wave of its baton, this virtuoso effortlessly brings order to arrays and vectors alike:

But wait! For those with an ear for the unconventional, our maestro unveils a stunning encore – descending order. By introducing a cunning companion, the

greater()

function, our maestro flips the script and brings the house down:

Yet the Sorting Serenade offers more than meets the ear. Venture deeper into the hallowed halls of custom comparators, and you'll find a bespoke experience tailored to your every whim. With a deft touch, you can define your own comparison functions to create a truly unique masterpiece:

Bubble Sort

Greetings, fellow coding enthusiasts! Today, we shall embark on a journey through the fascinating world of Bubble Sort, a popular sorting algorithm that will sweep you off your feet (but, hopefully, not your chair). It's time to pop some bubbles, folks! So, buckle up, grab your favorite caffeinated beverage, and let's get started.

Bubble Sort, affectionately known as the "sinking sort," is a simple yet elegant sorting algorithm. It works by repeatedly stepping through the list, comparing each adjacent pair of elements, and swapping them if they are in the wrong order. Over time, the smaller elements "bubble" to the front, while the larger ones "sink" to the bottom. See? It's just like making fizzy concoctions with a soda maker (or a mad scientist's laboratory, if you prefer).

Without further ado, let's dive into the nitty-gritty of Bubble Sort in C++.

Ah, isn't it a sight to behold? Let's break down this glorious chunk of code.

1. The function bubbleSort accepts a vector of integers called arr, which is passed by reference, so any changes we make to it will be reflected in the original vector.
2. We obtain the size of the vector using the size() function and store it in an integer variable called n.
3. The swapped boolean variable is used to keep track of whether any elements were swapped during each pass.
4. The outer loop iterates from 0 to n - 2, while the inner loop iterates from 0 to n - i - 2. Notice how we cleverly avoid redundant comparisons by shortening the inner loop with each iteration. Efficiency at its finest!
5. If the current element, arr[j], is greater than the next element, arr[j + 1], we swap them using the swap() function. This is the very essence of Bubble Sort - like a graceful dance of numbers.
6. If no elements were swapped during a complete pass, it means the list is already sorted, and we can break out of the loop early.

Voilà! You've just witnessed the magic of Bubble Sort. It's true that Bubble Sort isn't the fastest algorithm in the Sorting Kingdom (with its O(n^2) average and worst-case time complexity), but it sure is a great way to pop into the world of sorting algorithms. The simplicity and ease of understanding make Bubble Sort an excellent starting point for any budding programmer. So, go forth and spread the bubbly joy of Bubble Sort to the masses!

Greetings once more, my fellow code-slinging compadres! Today, we shall venture into the realm of Selection Sort, an enchanting sorting algorithm that's bound to pique your curiosity. It's time to unleash your inner Sorting Sorcerer and embark on a magical quest to vanquish disarray! Grab your wizard hat, code-scroll, and let's get sorting.

Selection Sort, often considered the "picky cousin" of Bubble Sort, is another simple and easy-to-understand sorting algorithm. It works its magic by iterating through the list, repeatedly selecting the smallest (or largest, depending on the order) element from the unsorted part of the list, and swapping it with the first unsorted element. In the end, the elements are sorted like a deck of cards, one by one.

Now, let's unravel the arcane secrets of Selection Sort in C++.

Behold, the mystical incantation of Selection Sort! Let's decode this beguiling snippet of sorcery.

1. The function selectionSort accepts a vector of integers called arr, which is passed by reference, ensuring that our magical transformations apply to the original vector.

2. We capture the size of the vector using the size() function and store it in an integer variable named n.
3. The integer variable min_index shall store the index of the smallest element found in each iteration.
4. The outer loop iterates from 0 to n - 2. The inner loop begins its journey at i + 1 and continues to n - 1.
5. As the inner loop progresses, we compare arr[j] with arr[min_index]. If we find a smaller element, we update min_index with the new index, j.
6. After the inner loop completes, if min_index is different from i, we swap the elements at the indices i and min_index using the swap() function.

And there you have it! The arcane art of Selection Sort revealed. While it may not be the most powerful algorithm in the Sorting Pantheon (it also boasts an O(n^2) average and worst-case time complexity), Selection Sort is a fantastic way to dip your toes into the enchanting waters of sorting algorithms. Its simplicity and charm will undoubtedly cast a spell on any aspiring code wizard. So, go forth, young Sorting Sorcerer, and may your selection be as swift as a shooting star!

Hear ye, hear ye, coding wizards and sorceresses! Gather 'round as we embark on a thrilling journey to explore the mythical land of Quick Sort, a realm filled with dazzling performance and magical partitioning. Prepare to have your minds blown, for we shall uncover the legendary secrets of a sorting algorithm that stands tall among its brethren. Fasten your seat belts, grab your enchanted keyboards, and let's dive into the mystical world of Quick Sort!

Quick Sort, a spellbinding algorithm conjured by the great Sir Tony Hoare in 1959, has since become one of the most widely used and celebrated sorting algorithms in the coding universe. Its magnificent power lies in its divide and conquer approach, which artfully slices the problem into smaller, more manageable pieces, much like a magical pizza cutter of efficiency.

Before we summon the C++ incantation of Quick Sort, let's decrypt its arcane mechanics. The algorithm operates by selecting a 'pivot' element from the array and partitioning the other elements into two groups: those less than the pivot and those greater than the pivot. This process is then recursively applied to the two subarrays, ultimately resulting in a fully sorted array.

And now, my fellow code-wielders, behold the enigmatic Quick Sort spell in C++:

Let us decipher this mesmerizing code snippet:

1. The partition function takes a reference to the arr vector, along with low and high indices, and returns the index of the pivot element after partitioning.
2. We initialize the pivot as the last element of the array, and i as low - 1.
3. As we traverse the array from low to high - 1, we compare each element with the pivot. If it's less than the pivot, we increment i and swap the elements at indices i and j.
4. After the loop, we swap the pivot element with the element at index i + 1, thus completing the partitioning.
5. The quickSort function calls the partition function to obtain the pivot index pi, then recursively applies itself to the two subarrays.

With a blazing average and best-case time complexity of $O(n \log n)$, the magnificent Quick Sort reigns supreme in the Sorting Kingdom. However, a word of caution to the intrepid coder: its worst-case time complexity is $O(n^2)$, which may arise when the chosen pivot is consistently the smallest or largest element. But fear not, for there are ways to mitigate this, such as choosing a random pivot or utilizing the "median of three" method.

So, go forth, valiant coders, and harness the power of Quick Sort to bring order to your digital realm! May your pivots be wise, your partitions precise, and your sorting swift as the wind!

Greetings, noble code artisans! Gather 'round, as we embark on an epic adventure through the fabled land of Merge Sort, a mystical domain where the ancient art of divide and conquer reigns supreme. Join us on this exhilarating quest to uncover the revered secrets of an algorithm that has enchanted programmers for generations. So, don your wizard hats, summon your enchanted keyboards, and let us unravel the enigmatic Merge Sort!

Hailing from the enchanted realm of computer algorithms, Merge Sort was first conjured by the illustrious sorcerer John von Neumann in 1945. Since then, it has become a celebrated sorting spell, revered for its stability and efficiency. Merge Sort's wondrous power lies in its masterful divide and conquer approach, cleaving problems into smaller, more manageable pieces, like a mage's enchanted blade slicing through the fabric of complexity.

But enough of the preamble! Let us now unveil the sacred C++ incantation of Merge Sort:

Behold this majestic code snippet, and let us decrypt its arcane mechanics:

1. The merge function takes a reference to the arr vector, along with left, mid, and right

indices. Its purpose is to merge two sorted subarrays into a single sorted subarray.

2. We create two temporary vectors, leftArr and rightArr, to store the elements of the left and right subarrays.

3. We then traverse both temporary vectors simultaneously, comparing their elements and inserting the smaller one back into the original array.

4. Finally, we copy any remaining elements from the temporary vectors back into the original array.

5. The mergeSort function divides the array recursively until we reach single-element subarrays. At that point, it calls the merge function to combine the sorted subarrays.

Merge Sort, with its awe-inspiring O(n log n) time complexity, has become a true legend in the Sorting Kingdom, revered by code adepts across the realm. Its enchanting stability ensures that equal elements maintain their original order, casting a spell of tranquility over your digital dominion.

So, noble coders, wield the mighty Merge Sort to bring harmony and order to your digital realm!

And so, our lyrical journey through the Sorting Serenade comes to a crescendo. With the power of C++ and the grace of the

sort()

function, you too can join the ranks of the algorithmic virtuosos, weaving your own tales of ordered arrays and melodious vectors. So, don your cape, grab your baton, and let the symphony begin!

Exercises: Sorting Serenade: Harmonizing Arrays and Vectors with C++

1. Name the two most commonly used sorting algorithms in C++'s Standard Library.

   Answer: The two most commonly used sorting algorithms in C++'s Standard Library are
   std::sort()
   and
   std::stable_sort()
   .

2. Write a C++ code snippet that sorts a vector of integers in ascending order using
   std::sort()
   .

3. What is the time complexity of the
   std::sort()
   function?

Answer: The time complexity of std::sort() is O(n log n), where n is the number of elements being sorted.

4. Write a C++ function that sorts a vector of strings in descending order using
   std::sort()
   .

5. How do you sort a vector of custom objects based on a specific attribute using std::sort()?

You can use a custom comparison function or a lambda function as the third argument of std::sort(). This function should take two objects as arguments and return a boolean value that represents the desired sorting order. For example:

6. Question: What is the main difference between std::sort() and std::stable_sort()?

Answer: The main difference is that

std::stable_sort()

maintains the relative order of elements with equal values, while

std::sort()

does not guarantee this.

7. Question: Write a C++ code snippet that sorts an array of integers in descending order using std::sort()

.

8. How can you sort a

std::list
of integers in ascending order?

Answer: You can use the member function std::list::sort() to sort the list in ascending order. For example:

9. How do you use std::partial_sort() to find the k smallest elements in a vector of integers?

Answer: You can use std::partial_sort() to sort the first k elements in the vector. For example:

10. How can you use `std::sort()` to sort a vector of integers based on their absolute values?

Answer: You can use a custom comparison function or a lambda function as the third argument of `std::sort()`. This function should take two integers as arguments and return a boolean value that represents the desired sorting order based on their absolute values. For example:

library, where the intrepid linear search, embodied by the

find()

function, bravely scours arrays and vectors alike, leaving no stone unturned:

However, for those seeking greater efficiency and a swifter resolution to their quest, a more refined approach beckons. Enter the enigmatic binary search, a master of divide and conquer, cutting search times like a hot knife through butter:

With the assistance of binary search, our journey's pace quickens, and the trail grows warmer. Yet, our enigmatic expedition does not end here, for the true adventurer craves not only discovery but also knowledge. With the

lower_bound()

and

upper_bound()

functions in our arsenal, we can ascertain the very boundaries of our search:

Writing Your Own Binary Search

Greetings, gallant seekers of coding knowledge! Today, we embark on an enthralling quest to uncover the arcane secrets of crafting a Binary Search from scratch, without the aid of any C++ libraries. Sit back, as I regale you with tales of algorithmic sorcery, and brace yourselves for a thrilling journey through the mystical realm of computer science.

Binary Search, a magical algorithmic incantation, has long been known to bestow upon its wielders the power to locate elements within sorted arrays or containers with unparalleled efficiency. By harnessing the mystical forces of divide and conquer, Binary Search has proven time and time again its ability to vanquish complexity, casting it into the abyss of O(log n) runtime.

Fear not, dear adventurers, for you too can learn to wield the power of Binary Search! Behold, the sacred C++ incantation to create a custom Binary Search:

Let us now decode this mystical incantation, deciphering the arcane mechanisms that lie at the heart of Binary Search:

1. We initialize two pointers,
   left
   and
   right
   , to represent the boundaries of the search space within the array.
2. As long as
   left
   remains less than or equal to
   right
   , the search space is not empty, and our quest continues.
3. We calculate the midpoint,
   mid
   , of the search space, taking care not to summon the dreaded Integer Overflow demon.

4. If the target element is found at the midpoint, our quest is complete, and we return the index.
5. If the target element is greater than the midpoint value, we adjust the left boundary to the right of the midpoint.
6. If the target element is less than the midpoint value, we adjust the right boundary to the left of the midpoint.
7. Should our search prove fruitless, we return -1, signifying that the elusive element remains hidden.

Armed with this powerful incantation, you now possess the ability to craft your very own Binary Search. No longer shall you be shackled by the constraints of C++ libraries, as you venture forth into the realm of algorithmic mastery!

So, brave code wizards, go forth and conquer! Wield the mighty Binary Search to vanquish inefficiency and bring order to your digital dominion. May your quest be filled with triumph and joy, and may your algorithmic prowess grow with each passing day!

And so, the curtain falls on our enigmatic expedition. With a trusty array or vector by our side and the power of C++ search guiding our way, we venture forth into uncharted territories, uncovering lost elements and unearthing hidden knowledge. Onward, to adventure!

1. What is the difference between linear search and binary search?

Answer: Linear search is a simple search algorithm that iterates through each element in a collection until it finds the desired element or reaches the end. Its time complexity is O(n), where n is the size of the collection. Binary search is a more efficient search algorithm that works on sorted collections. It repeatedly divides the search interval in half until it finds the desired element or the interval becomes empty. Its time complexity is O(log n).

2. Write a function that performs a linear search on a given vector and returns the index of the first occurrence of a given value. If the value is not found, return -1.
3. Write a function that performs a binary search on a given sorted vector and returns the index of the given value. If the value is not found, return -1.
4. Can binary search be used on an unsorted vector?

Answer: No, binary search requires the input vector to be sorted. If the vector is unsorted, using binary search will lead to incorrect results. You must sort the vector before applying binary search, or use a different search method like linear search.

5. What is the time complexity of searching for an element in a sorted vector using the std::lower_bound() function?

Answer: The time complexity of

std::lower_bound()

is O(log n), where n is the size of the vector. It uses binary search to find the first occurrence of the given element or the position where the element would be inserted to maintain the sorted order.

6. Write a code snippet that finds the first occurrence of the value 42 in a sorted std::vector called numbers using std::lower_bound()

.

7. What is the time complexity of searching for an element in an unordered_set ?

The average time complexity of searching for an element in an

std::unordered_set

is O(1). However, in the worst case, it can be O(n), where n is the size of the unordered_set.

8. Can you use binary search on a linked list? Why or why not?

No. Binary search requires random access to elements in a collection, which means you can access any element in constant time. However, a linked list does not provide constant-time random access to elements because each element is only accessible by traversing the list starting from the head node.

As a result, binary search cannot be directly applied to a singly-linked list in its standard form.

To use binary search on a linked list, you would need to modify the standard binary search algorithm to work with a linked list by keeping track of the mid-point of the list and traversing the list accordingly. This would require finding the length of the list, which would take linear time, and then performing binary search by traversing the list in O(log n) time.

Therefore, while it is possible to use binary search on a linked list, it would not be efficient as compared to other data structures such as an array or a balanced binary search tree.

The Adventures of Simulation & Brute Force: Tales of Complete Search in C++

Greetings, code-knights and algorithm aficionados! Gather 'round as we regale you with the thrilling tales of Simulation and Brute Force, the dynamic duo of Complete Search in the magical realm of C++. With ingenuity and perseverance, they conquer even the most perplexing of problems.

Simulation, the cunning strategist, devises models to mimic real-world scenarios, calculating outcomes with impeccable precision:

Fear not, for Brute Force is ever at the ready, with an unyielding spirit and unwavering determination to explore every possible solution:

Though they embark on separate quests, our heroes ultimately reunite in the fabled land of Complete Search, combining their powers to achieve the seemingly impossible:

With their tales of valor and triumph, Simulation and Brute Force have become the stuff of legend. In the ever-enchanting world of C++, their legacy lives on, inspiring generations of code-knights and algorithm aficionados to forge their own paths and embark on thrilling quests of their own. To adventure and beyond!

1. What is a brute force (complete search) algorithm?

Answer: A brute force (complete search) algorithm is an approach where all possible solutions to a problem are generated and checked to find the correct solution. This method is usually simple to implement but can be inefficient, especially for large input sizes.

2. What is the time complexity of a brute force algorithm that checks all combinations of N elements?

Answer: The time complexity of a brute force algorithm that checks all combinations of N elements is usually $O(2^N)$ since it explores all possible subsets of the input set. However, the complexity may vary depending on the specific problem and implementation.

3. Write a function that finds the maximum sum subarray of a given vector using a brute force approach.

4. Describe a situation where using a brute force algorithm would be appropriate.

Answer: A brute force algorithm is appropriate when the input size is small, the problem's solution space is not too large, or when you need a quick and easy-to-implement solution to verify the correctness of a more efficient algorithm.

5. Write a function that checks if a given string is a palindrome using a brute force approach.
6. Write a brute force algorithm to find the greatest common divisor (GCD) of two integers.
7. Given a list of integers, find all the subsets that have a sum equal to a target value using a brute force approach.
8. Write a brute force algorithm to find the longest common subsequence (LCS) of two strings.
9. Using a brute force approach, find the number of ways to make change for a given amount using a set of coin denominations.
10. What are the main disadvantages of using brute force algorithms?

Answer: The main disadvantages of brute force algorithms are their inefficiency and poor performance, especially for large input sizes. Brute force algorithms often have high time and/or space complexity, which makes them impractical for solving real-world problems with large inputs. However, they can be useful for small inputs or when used to verify the correctness of a more efficient algorithm.

Greedy Algorithms: The Swift, the Smart, and the Validated

Ahoy, fellow coding connoisseurs and algorithm adventurers! Lend us your ears, for we bring you the tale of a cunning strategist – the Greedy Algorithm. Known for its swiftness and keen intellect, Greedy always seizes the most alluring option at each step, hoping to secure the ultimate treasure.

But beware, for Greedy's ways can lead to a slippery slope. To validate whether Greedy's choices are sound, we must ensure that the problem possesses two essential properties: Greedy Choice Property and Optimal Substructure.

The Greedy Choice Property states that the globally optimal solution can be constructed from locally optimal choices. This means that at each step, Greedy's choice will not affect the final outcome.

Optimal Substructure is the idea that an optimal solution can be constructed from optimal solutions of its subproblems. If a problem can be broken down into smaller parts, and optimal solutions for those parts can be combined to form the optimal solution for the original problem, we have an optimal substructure.

Greetings, coding aficionados! Today, we shall embark on a daring quest to master the subtle art of being greedy, treading the fine line between clever optimization and reckless abandon. With great power comes great responsibility, and the greedy algorithm is no exception. So, let us proceed with caution as we unravel the mysteries of choosing and validating greedy approaches.

The greedy approach, like a mischievous trickster, can entice us with the promise of swift and effortless solutions. However, beware its cunning ways! For although it may lead to glory in some cases, it can also lure us into a trap of suboptimal outcomes. Before we succumb to its seductive allure, we must first ask ourselves: "Is this truly the path to victory, or merely a clever ruse?"

Fear not, dear coders, for there is a way to see through the deception: validation. When confronted with the tantalizing prospect of a greedy solution, consider the following steps to validate its viability:

1. Prove it: Use mathematical induction or some other proof technique to demonstrate that the greedy choice results in an optimal solution. Show that, at each step, making the greediest choice leads to the desired outcome.
2. Counterexample: If a greedy approach seems too good to be true, it might be! Seek out

counterexamples to test its mettle. If you can find even a single case where the greedy strategy fails, it's time to bid it farewell and search for a more reliable solution.

3. Problem structure: Analyze the problem's structure for clues. Some problems lend themselves naturally to greedy solutions, while others are more resistant. Consider whether the problem exhibits properties like the greedy-choice property or optimal substructure, which can signal that a greedy approach is indeed suitable.

4. Experience: As you traverse the realm of competitive programming, you'll encounter countless greedy algorithms in the wild. Learn from these examples, and use your newfound wisdom to identify when a greedy approach is a wise choice, and when it's best to steer clear.

So there you have it, noble coders – the path to validating greedy approaches in all their tantalizing complexity. As you venture forth into the world of algorithms, may your discernment and intuition guide you to make the right choices, and may your code flow as smoothly as a perfectly executed greedy strategy.

Exercises: Greedy Algorithms: The Swift, the Smart, and the Validated

1. What is a greedy algorithm?

Answer: A greedy algorithm is a problem-solving approach that makes the locally optimal choice at each step with the hope of finding a globally optimal solution. It focuses on making the best possible decision at each stage, without considering the overall problem or future consequences.

2. Mention a popular problem where a greedy algorithm provides an optimal solution.

Answer: The popular problem where a greedy algorithm provides an optimal solution is the "Fractional Knapsack Problem". In this problem, we have a knapsack with a given capacity and a set of items with different weights and values. The objective is to maximize the total value of the items in the knapsack, and we are allowed to take fractions of the items.

3. Explain the greedy algorithm for the fractional knapsack problem.

Answer: The greedy algorithm for the fractional knapsack problem is as follows:

- Calculate the value per unit weight (value/weight) for each item.
- Sort the items in descending order based on their value per unit weight.
- Select items from the sorted list until the knapsack is full, taking as much of each item as possible.

4. Write a C++ function to implement the greedy algorithm for the fractional knapsack problem.
5. Can greedy algorithms always guarantee an optimal solution?

Answer: No, greedy algorithms cannot always guarantee an optimal solution. They work well for certain problems, like the fractional knapsack problem, but may produce suboptimal solutions for other problems, such as the 0/1 knapsack problem or the traveling salesman problem.

6. Explain the greedy algorithm for the coin change problem.

Answer: The greedy algorithm for the coin change problem is as follows:

- Sort the coin denominations in descending order.
- Start with the largest denomination and use as many coins as possible without exceeding the target amount.
- Move to the next largest denomination and repeat the process until the target amount is reached or there are no more denominations left.

7. Does the greedy algorithm for the coin change problem always produce the minimum number of coins required?

Answer: No, the greedy algorithm for the coin change problem does not always produce the minimum number of coins required. It works well for certain sets of coin denominations, like the U.S. coin system, but may produce suboptimal solutions for other sets of denominations.

8. What are some advantages of using greedy algorithms?

Answer: Some advantages of using greedy algorithms are their simplicity, ease of implementation, and relatively lower time complexity compared to other algorithms. They can often provide a good approximate solution to a problem, even if it is not guaranteed to be optimal.

9. Implement a greedy algorithm to find the minimum number of intervals needed to cover a given set of intervals.

10. Explain the activity selection problem and how a greedy algorithm can be used to solve it.

Answer: The activity selection problem involves choosing the maximum number of non-overlapping activities that can be performed, given a set of activities with start and end times. A greedy algorithm can be used to solve this problem by selecting activities based on their earliest finishing times. The algorithm sorts the activities by their end times and iterativel

Recursion: Unraveling the Magical Loops of Code

Greetings, esteemed code magicians and algorithm aficionados! Gather 'round and prepare to be mesmerized by the enchanted world of Recursion. A spellbinding technique that conjures solutions from the depths of nested functions, Recursion is the spell you never knew you needed!

But beware, young wizards, for with great power comes great responsibility. To wield the mighty force of Recursion, you must understand its inner workings. Fear not, for we shall guide you through the enchanted forest of recursive thinking!

Recursion is built upon two mystical pillars: the base case and the recursive case. The base case is the simplest form of the problem, a condition that halts the recursive calls and returns a value. The recursive case is where the magic happens, invoking the function itself with a smaller version of the problem.

Now, to validate that a greedy algorithm is the optimal solution to a recursive problem, we must ensure that the problem possesses the two essential properties we previously discussed: Greedy Choice Property and Optimal Substructure.

Remember, the Greedy Choice Property ensures that the globally optimal solution can be constructed from locally optimal choices. The Optimal Substructure confirms that an optimal solution can be built from optimal solutions of its subproblems.

However, keep in mind that not all recursive problems can be solved optimally using a greedy approach. In such cases, dynamic programming or other techniques may be the key to unlocking the optimal solution.

So, gather your wands and prepare to embark on an extraordinary journey through the enchanted world of Recursion. Hone your skills, young wizards, and let the magic of code guide you toward the realm of untold power and infinite possibilities!

The Recursive Rabbit Hole: Venturing Forth with Wisdom and Wit

Today, we shall navigate the winding, spiraling depths of recursion, exploring its tantalizing twists and turns. Recursion, that enigmatic and mind-bending beast, can be both a blessing and a curse. So, let us ponder the good and the bad, the light and the dark, and discern when recursion is the key to enlightenment or a gateway to doom.

The Good:

1. Elegance: When the planets align and the stars shine bright, recursion can weave its magic and transform complex problems into simple, elegant solutions. Beauty lies in brevity, and recursive code can often achieve this elusive ideal.

2. Intuitive: Sometimes, a problem simply begs for recursion. When a problem exhibits a natural hierarchical structure or can be broken down into smaller, identical subproblems, recursion can be as natural and intuitive as breathing.

The Bad:

1. Stack Overflow: Alas, recursion's Achilles' heel: the dreaded stack overflow! Should your function call itself one too many times, you risk toppling the Jenga tower of function calls and crashing your program into oblivion.
2. Efficiency: While recursion can be a thing of beauty, it can also be slow and inefficient. Repeatedly solving the same subproblems can lead to exponential time complexity, which, as we all know, is a coder's worst nightmare.

Now that we've weighed the pros and cons, let's consider when to embrace recursion's sweet siren song and when to resist its tempting embrace:

When to use recursion:

1. The problem can be naturally divided into smaller, identical subproblems.
2. A non-recursive solution is excessively complex or hard to comprehend.
3. The depth of recursion is manageable and unlikely to cause a stack overflow.

When to avoid recursion:

1. The problem can be solved more efficiently with an iterative approach.
2. The depth of recursion is too great, increasing the risk of stack overflow.
3. Recursion introduces unnecessary complexity, making the code harder to understand and maintain.

There you have it, dear coders – a guide to help you traverse the labyrinth of recursion with wisdom and grace. May your code be elegant, your stack overflow-free, and your recursive adventures full of triumph and discovery!

Exercises: Recursion: Unraveling the Magical Loops of Code

1. What is recursion in C++?

Answer: Recursion is a programming technique where a function calls itself in order to solve a smaller version of the same problem. This process continues until a base case is reached, which is the simplest version of the problem that can be solved directly.

2. Write a recursive function to calculate the factorial of a non-negative integer

   n

   .

3. Write a recursive function to compute the nth Fibonacci number.

4. Explain the difference between direct and indirect recursion.

Answer: Direct recursion occurs when a function calls itself directly within its body, while indirect recursion occurs when a function calls another function, which in turn calls the first function.

5. How can you avoid stack overflow in a recursive function?

Answer: To avoid stack overflow in a recursive function, you can use techniques such as memoization to store intermediate results, or rewrite the function using an iterative approach instead of recursion.

6. Write a recursive function to find the greatest common divisor (GCD) of two integers using the Euclidean algorithm.
7. Write a recursive function to calculate the sum of an array of integers.
8. Write a recursive function to reverse a string.
9. Explain tail recursion and how it is different from regular recursion.

Answer: Tail recursion is a special case of recursion where the recursive call is the last operation in the function. In tail recursion, the compiler can optimize the function by reusing the existing stack frame, eliminating the need for additional stack frames. This can lead to improved performance and reduced memory usage compared to regular recursion.

10. Write a recursive function to find the height of a binary tree.

The Adventure Continues: Your Next Steps in Competitive Programming

Bravo, brave code warriors! You've embarked on an incredible journey through the treacherous terrains of USACO preparation and emerged victorious. We've traversed through the valleys of C++ programming, climbed the peaks of data structures, and unraveled the mysteries of algorithms. But, as with any epic adventure, this is merely the beginning!

The world of competitive coding is vast, and limitless opportunities await you. As you venture forth, remember that knowledge is your greatest weapon, and practice is your trusty steed. Keep honing your skills, sharpening your algorithms, and refining your strategies. The road to USACO mastery may be long and challenging, but fear not, for you have already proven your mettle and are well-equipped to conquer whatever lies ahead.

To fuel your ever-growing thirst for coding knowledge, we recommend visiting the enchanted realm of usaco.fun. This magical portal offers a myriad of coding challenges and resources, all designed to make your learning experience not only rewarding but also delightful. After all, who said coding couldn't be fun?

At usaco.fun, you will find an ever-growing collection of coding challenges that will test your abilities, expand your horizons, and keep your grey matter sharp. The platform offers engaging tutorials, practice problems, and real-life examples that will make even the most arcane algorithms feel like a walk in the park. So, saddle up and embark on this exciting new journey to learn coding the fun way!

Remember, young code wizards, the pursuit of knowledge is a never-ending quest. Stay curious, stay passionate, and never stop exploring the vast and wondrous world of competitive programming. May the spirit of code be with you, and may you continue to conquer the digital realm with confidence and flair.

Now, go forth and code! The world awaits your brilliance!

Solutions

Solutions: Say Hello to C++: Your First 'Hello, World!' Program

1. What is the purpose of the main() function in a C++ program?

Answer: The main() function is the entry point of a C++ program. When the program is executed, the main() function is called first, and the code inside the function is executed sequentially.

Solutions: C++ Variables Unleashed: Naming, Changing, and Taming the Constants

1. Question: What are the rules for naming variables in C++?

Answer: The rules for naming variables in C++ are:

```
Variable names must start with a letter or an
underscore (_).
They can contain letters, digits, and undersc
ores.
Variable names are case-sensitive.
They must not be C++ reserved keywords.
```

Explanation: Following these rules ensures that variable names are unique, easily recognizable, and do not conflict with reserved keywords.

2. Question: How do you declare a variable in C++?

Answer: To declare a variable in C++, you need to specify the data type followed by the variable name. Optionally, you can also assign an initial value.

Example:

Explanation: In the example, we declare an integer variable named my_number and a float variable named my_float initialized with the value 3.14. The variable names must follow the naming conventions and should not conflict with reserved keywords.

3. Question: What is the purpose of the const keyword?

Answer: The const keyword is used to declare a constant variable, which cannot be modified after its initialization.

Example:

Explanation: In the example, we declare a constant integer variable named days_in_week and initialize it with the value 7. Once initialized, the value of this variable cannot be changed during the program execution, ensuring that the value remains constant throughout the program.

4. Question: What is the difference between assignment and initialization in C++?

Answer: Initialization sets a variable's value when it is declared, while assignment assigns a new value to an existing variable.

Example:

Explanation: In the example, the variable a is initialized with the value 5 when it is declared. Later, its value is updated through assignment with the new value 10.

5. Question: Can you assign a value of one data type to a variable of another data type in C++? Explain with an example.

Answer: Yes, you can assign a value of one data type to a variable of another data type, but it may result in data loss or truncation if the target data type cannot represent the full range or precision of the source data type.

Example:

Explanation: In this example, an integer value 3 is assigned to a float variable my_float. The assignment is allowed, and the value of my_float will be 3.0. However, if the source data type has a larger range or higher precision than the target data type, the value might be truncated or lose precision during the assignment.

6. Question: What is the syntax for declaring multiple variables of the same data type in a single line?

Answer: To declare multiple variables of the same data type in a single line, use a comma-separated list of variable names after the data type.

Example:

Explanation: In the example, three integer variables x, y, and z are declared in a single line. This is a more concise way to declare multiple variables of the same data type.

7. Question: What happens if you use an uninitialized variable in C++?

Answer: Using an uninitialized variable in C++ can lead to undefined behavior, as the variable may contain a garbage value.

Explanation: When a variable is declared without initialization, its value is not set to a default value, and it contains whatever data was previously stored at that memory location. Using uninitialized variables can result in unpredictable behavior and hard-to-find bugs in your program. It is always a good practice to initialize variables before using them.

1. Question: What are the two types of comments in C++?

Answer: The two types of comments in C++ are:

- Single-line comments: They start with
  //
  and continue to the end of the line.
- Multi-line comments: They start with
  /*
  and end with
  */
  .

Explanation: Single-line comments are used for short explanations or to temporarily disable a line of code, while multi-line comments are used for longer explanations or to disable multiple lines of code at once.

2. Question: How do you write a single-line comment in C++?

Answer: To write a single-line comment in C++, start the comment with

//

followed by the comment text.

Example:

Explanation: In the example, the text following // is a single-line comment, and it does not affect the execution of the code.

3. Question: How do you write a multi-line comment in C++?

Answer: To write a multi-line comment in C++, start the comment with

/*

and end it with

*/

.

Example:

Explanation: In the example, the text between /* and */ is a multi-line comment, and it does not affect the execution of the code. Multi-line comments can span multiple lines of text.

4. Question: Can comments be nested in C++?

Answer: Single-line comments can be nested within multi-line comments, but multi-line comments cannot be nested within each other.

Example:

Explanation: In the example, the single-line comment is nested within the multi-line comment, which is allowed. However, attempting to nest a multi-line comment within another multi-line comment will result in a syntax error.

5. Question: What is the purpose of comments in C++ code?

Answer: The purpose of comments in C++ code is to:

- Explain the purpose and functionality of the code.
- Make the code more readable and understandable for others or for yourself when revisiting the code later.
- Temporarily disable a line or block of code during debugging or testing.

Explanation: Comments are not executed by the compiler and do not affect the functionality of the code. They serve as a means to document and explain the code to make it easier for others to understand or to remind yourself of how the code works when revisiting it later. Additionally, comments can be used to temporarily disable parts of the code during debugging or testing.

Solutions: C++ Data Types: The Building Blocks of Code Alchemy

1. Question: What are the four primary data types in C++?

Answer: The four primary data types in C++ are:

- int (integer)
- float (floating-point number)
- double (double-precision floating-point number)
- char (character)

Explanation: These data types are used to represent different kinds of data in a C++ program. Integers are whole numbers, floats and doubles are used for real numbers (doubles provide more precision than floats), and chars represent single characters.

2. Question: What is the difference between a float and a double in C++?

Answer: The main difference between a float and a double in C++ is the precision and range they can represent. Floats have single-precision, while doubles have double-precision, which means that doubles can represent a larger range and more accurate values than floats.

Explanation: Floats use 4 bytes of memory and typically have a precision of about 6-7 decimal digits, while doubles use 8 bytes of memory and have a precision of about 15-17 decimal digits. This increased precision allows doubles to represent larger numbers and more accurate decimal values than floats.

3. Question: How do you declare a variable with a specific data type in C++?

Answer: To declare a variable with a specific data type in C++, you need to specify the data type followed by the variable name. Optionally, you can also assign a value to the variable during declaration.

Example:

Explanation: In the example, four variables are declared with different data types: an int, a float, a double, and a char. Each variable is assigned an initial value during declaration.

4. Question: What is the purpose of the sizeof()
operator in C++?

Answer: The

sizeof()

operator in C++ is used to determine the size (in bytes) of a data type or a variable of a specific data type.

Example:

Explanation: In the example, the

sizeof()

operator is used to display the size of the int data type and the size of the myInt

variable. Both values will be the same, as

myInt

is of type int.

5. Question: What is the difference between
    signed and unsigned integer types in C++?

Answer: The main difference between signed and
unsigned integer types in C++ is that signed integers
can represent both positive and negative values,
while unsigned integers can only represent non-
negative values.

Explanation: Signed integers use one bit to represent
the sign of the number, while the remaining bits
represent the magnitude. Unsigned integers use all
bits to represent the magnitude, allowing for a larger
range of positive values but not allowing for negative
values. For example, an unsigned 8-bit integer can
represent values from 0 to 255, while a signed 8-bit
integer can represent values from -128 to 127.

6. Question: What are the basic data types in
    C++?

Answer: The basic data types in C++ are int, float,
double, char, and bool.

Explanation: These data types represent different
types of data, such as integers, floating-point
numbers, characters, and boolean values (true or

false). They are used to declare variables in C++ programs.

7. Question: What is the difference between int and float data types?

Answer: int is used for storing integer values, while float is used for storing floating-point numbers.

Explanation: Integer values are whole numbers without a decimal part, while floating-point numbers have both an integer part and a decimal part. The int data type uses less memory and is generally faster for arithmetic operations compared to float.

8. Question: What is the purpose of the bool data type?

Answer: The bool data type is used to represent boolean values, either true or false.

Explanation: Boolean values are used in conditional expressions and control structures, such as if statements and loops. They are the result of logical and comparison operations.

Solutions: C++ Mathemagics: Conjuring Calculations and Casting Spells"

1. Question: What are the basic arithmetic operators in C++?

Answer: The basic arithmetic operators in C++ are:

• Addition: +

- Subtraction: -
- Multiplication: *
- Division: /
- Modulus (remainder): %

Explanation: These operators allow you to perform basic arithmetic operations on numeric values in a C++ program. They can be used with integer, float, and double data types.

2. Question: What is the difference between integer division and floating-point division in C++?

Answer: In C++, integer division truncates any decimal portion of the result, while floating-point division retains the decimal portion.

Example:

Explanation: In the example, when dividing two integers, the decimal portion is truncated, resulting in an integer value. When dividing a float by an integer, floating-point division is performed, and the decimal portion is retained.

3. Question: Read the following code and determine its output:

Answer: The output of the code will be 1.

Explanation: The code calculates the remainder of the division of a (10) by b (3) using the modulus operator

(%). The remainder of 10 divided by 3 is 1, so the output will be 1.

4. Question: Write a C++ code snippet that calculates the area of a circle with a radius of 5.0 and displays the result. (Assume PI = 3.14159)

Answer:

Explanation: In this example, we declare a

double

variable

radius

with a value of 5.0, and a

double

constant

PI

with a value of 3.14159. We then calculate the area using the formula

area = PI * radius * radius

and display the result.

5. Question: What is the result of the following expression in C++?

Answer: The result of the expression will be

12

.

Explanation: Following the order of operations, the expression is evaluated as follows:

Thus, the value of

x

is

12

.

1. Question: What are the basic boolean (logical) operators in C++?

Answer: The basic boolean operators in C++ are:

```
AND: &&
OR:  ||
NOT: !
```

Explanation: These operators allow you to perform logical operations on boolean values in a C++ program. They can be used in conditional statements and loops to control the flow of the program based on the truthiness of certain conditions.

2. Question: What is the difference between the
    &&

(AND) and

||

(OR) operators in C++?

Answer: The && (AND) operator returns true if both operands are

true

, and

false

otherwise. The

||

(OR) operator returns

true

if at least one of the operands is

true

, and

false

otherwise.

Explanation: These operators are used to combine multiple boolean expressions in a C++ program. The

&&

operator is used when all conditions must be met, while the

||

operator is used when at least one of the conditions must be met.

3. Question: Read the following code and determine its output:

Answer: The output of the code will be 0.

Explanation: The code calculates the result of the boolean expression

a && b

using the AND operator (&&). Since

a

is true and

b

is

false

, the expression evaluates to

false

. In C++, boolean values are displayed as integers:

true

is displayed as 1, and

false

is displayed as

0

. Thus, the output will be

0

.

4. Question: Write a C++ code snippet that checks if a given integer x is positive and even, and displays "Yes" if it is, or "No" otherwise.

Answer:

Explanation: In this example, we declare an int variable x with a value of 4. We then use a conditional statement with the AND operator (&&) to check if x is positive (x > 0) and even (x % 2 == 0). If both conditions are true, we display "Yes", otherwise, we display "No".

5. Question: What is the result of the following boolean expression in C++?

Answer: The result of the expression will be

true

.

Explanation: Following the order of operations, the expression is evaluated as follows:

Thus, the value of

x

is

true

.

Solutions: C++ Control Flow Chronicles: Embarking on an If-Else Adventure

1. Question: What are the three basic conditional statements in C++?

Answer: The three basic conditional statements in C++ are:

```
if
if-else
if-else if-else
```

Explanation: Conditional statements are used to control the flow of a program based on specific conditions. The

if

statement checks if a single condition is

true

, the

if-else

statement checks if a condition is

true

and provides an alternative path if it is false, and the

if-else if-else

statement checks for multiple conditions and provides alternative paths for each condition.

2. Question: What is the purpose of the else
statement in C++?

Answer: The

else

statement provides an alternative path of execution when the condition in the preceding

if

statement is false.

Explanation: The

else

statement is used after an

if

statement to specify the code block that should be executed when the condition in the

if

statement is not met (

false

). It allows for more complex decision-making in a program.

3. Question: Read the following code and determine its output:

Answer: The output of the code will be Odd.

Explanation: The code checks if the remainder of

x

divided by 2 is equal to 0 using the modulo operator (%). If the condition is true, it means x is even, and the program outputs "Even". Otherwise, it means

x

is odd, and the program outputs "Odd". Since 7 is an odd number, the output will be "Odd".

4. Question: Write a C++ code snippet that reads an integer from the user and checks if it is positive, negative, or zero, displaying the appropriate message for each case.

Answer:

Explanation: In this example, we declare an

int

variable

x

and read its value from the user using cin. We then
use an

if-else if-else

statement to check if

x

is positive, negative, or zero, and display the
appropriate message for each case.

5. Question: What is the result of the following
   code?

Answer: The output of the code will be

x is greater

.

Explanation: The code checks if

x

is greater than or less than

y

using the

if-else if-else

statement. If

x > y

, it sets the result variable to "x is greater". If

x < y

, it sets the

result

variable to "y is greater". If x and y are equal

1. Question: What are the three types of loops in C++?

Answer: The three types of loops in C++ are:

```
for loop
while loop
do-while loop
```

Explanation: Loops are used to repeatedly execute a block of code until a specific condition is met. The

for

loop is used when the number of iterations is known, the

while

loop is used when the loop should continue as long as a given condition is

true

, and the

do-while

loop is used when the loop should execute at least once and continue as long as a given condition is

true

.

2. Question: Read the following code and determine its output:

Answer: The output of the code will be:

Explanation: The code uses a

for

loop to iterate from 1 to 5 (inclusive), printing the value of the loop variable

i

on each iteration.

3. Question: Write a C++ code snippet that reads a positive integer n from the user and calculates the factorial of

n

(n!) using a
while
loop.

Answer:

Explanation: In this example, we declare an

int

variable

n

and read its value from the user using

cin

. We then use a

while

loop to calculate the factorial of

n

and store the result in the

factorial

variable. Finally, we display the calculated factorial.

4.   Question: What is the purpose of the
     break
     statement in C++ loops?

Answer: The

break

statement is used to exit a loop prematurely, stopping its execution immediately.

Explanation: The

break

statement can be used inside a loop (for, while, or do-while) to immediately exit the loop when a certain condition is met. It is useful for cases when the loop should stop before the loop condition is false or before completing all iterations.

5. Question: What is the result of the following code?

Answer: The output of the code will be

Sum: 55

.

Explanation: The code uses a

while

loop to iterate from 1 to 10 (inclusive) and calculates the sum of all numbers from 1 to 10. The loop variable i is incremented on each iteration, and the value of i is added to the

sum

variable. After the loop is finished, the program displays the calculated sum, which is 55.

6. Question: What is a nested loop, and when is it used in C++?

Answer: A nested loop is a loop placed inside another loop. Nested loops are used when you need to perform a set of operations for each element in a sequence while also iterating through another sequence.

Explanation: Nested loops can be used for tasks that require iterating through multiple dimensions, such as processing matrices or multi-dimensional arrays, or when the number of iterations in an inner loop depends on the current value of the outer loop.

7. Question: Read the following code and determine its output:

Answer: The output of the code will be:

Explanation: The code uses two nested

for

loops to print a pattern of asterisks. The outer loop iterates three times, and for each iteration, the inner loop iterates i times, printing an asterisk. This results in a triangle pattern of asterisks.

8. Question: Write a C++ code snippet that reads a positive integer n from the user and prints a

pattern of numbers in the shape of an inverted triangle, like the following example for

n = 5

:

Answer:

Explanation: In this example, we declare an

int

variable n and read its value from the user using

cin

. We then use nested

for

loops to print the inverted triangle pattern of numbers. The outer loop iterates from n to 1 (inclusive), and the inner loop iterates from the current value of

i

down to

1

, printing the value of

j

on each iteration.

9. Question: What is the purpose of the

continue

statement in C++ loops, and how does it differ from the

break

statement?

Answer: The

continue

statement is used to skip the rest of the current iteration of a loop and move on to the next iteration. It differs from the

break

statement, which exits the loop entirely.

Explanation: The

continue

statement can be used inside a loop (for, while, or do-while) to skip the rest of the current iteration and proceed to the next iteration without executing the remaining statements in the loop body. Unlike the break statement, the continue statement does not exit the loop entirely; it only skips the current iteration.

10. Question: Read the following code and determine its output:

Answer: The output of the code will be:

Explanation: The code uses a

for

loop to iterate from 1 to 5.

1. Question: What is an array in C++, and why are arrays useful?

Answer: An array is a fixed-size, contiguous block of memory that stores multiple elements of the same data type. Arrays are useful for organizing and managing large amounts of data efficiently.

Explanation: Arrays provide a way to store multiple values of the same data type in a single variable, making it easier to work with and manipulate large sets of data. They are particularly useful when you need to perform operations on a sequence of elements, such as sorting or searching.

2. Question: How do you declare an array in C++?

Answer: To declare an array in C++, you specify the data type, followed by the array name, and then the size of the array in square brackets. For example:

int myArray[10]

;

Explanation: In this example, we declare an array named

myArray

with a size of 10 elements, all of which are of type int.

3. Question: How do you access elements of an array in C++?

Answer: You access elements of an array by using the array name followed by an index in square brackets. For example: myArray[3]

Explanation: In this example, we access the fourth element (since C++ uses zero-based indexing) of the myArray array.

4. Question: What is the range of valid indices for an array of size n in C++?

Answer: The range of valid indices for an array of size n is 0 to n-1.

Explanation: C++ uses zero-based indexing, so the first element of an array is at index 0, and the last element is at index n-1.

5. Question: Read the following code and determine its output:

Answer: The output of the code will be 12.

Explanation: The code accesses the second element of the array

arr

(which is 4) and the fourth element (which is 8), then adds them together, resulting in the output 12.

6. Question: Write a C++ code snippet that reads a positive integer

n

from the user, creates an array of size n, fills it with the first n even numbers, and then prints the sum of the array's elements.

Answer:

Explanation: In this example, we declare an

int

variable

n

, read its value from the user using

cin

, and then create an array of size

n

. We then use a

for

loop to fill the array with the first

n

even numbers and calculate the sum at the same time. Finally, we print the sum of the array's elements.

7. Question: What is the difference between a one-dimensional array and a two-dimensional array in C++?

Answer: A one-dimensional array stores elements in a single row or column, while a two-dimensional array

Solutions: C++ Vectors: The Shape-Shifting Magicians of Data Storage

1. Question: What is a vector in C++, and how does it differ from an array?

Answer: A vector is a dynamic, resizable array-like container provided by the C++ Standard Library. Unlike arrays, vectors can be resized during runtime, and their size can be changed as elements are added or removed.

Explanation: Vectors provide more flexibility compared to arrays, as they can be resized and offer various built-in functions to manage elements more easily.

2. Question: How do you include the necessary library to use
vectors
in C++?

Answer: To use vectors in C++, you must include the

header. For example:

#include

Explanation: The

header is part of the C++ Standard Library and provides the necessary definitions for the vector class template.

3. Question: How do you declare and initialize a vector in C++?

Answer: To declare and initialize a vector, you specify the vector keyword, followed by the data type in angle brackets, and then the vector name. You can optionally provide an initializer list to set the initial elements. For example:

vector myVector = {1, 2, 3, 4};

Explanation: In this example, we declare a vector named myVector that stores int elements and initializes it with the elements 1, 2, 3, and 4.

4. Question: How do you access elements of a vector in C++?

Answer: You can access elements of a vector using the [] operator with an index or by using the

at()

member function. For example:

myVector[1]

or

myVector.at(1)

Explanation: In both examples, we access the second element (since C++ uses zero-based indexing) of the

myVector

vector.

5. Question: What is the range of valid indices for a vector of size n in C++?

Answer: The range of valid indices for a vector of size n is 0 to n-1.

Explanation: Like arrays, C++ vectors use zero-based indexing, so the first element of a vector is at index 0, and the last element is at index n-1.

6. Question: Read the following code and determine its output:

Answer: The output of the code will be 12.

Explanation: The code accesses the second element of the vector

vec

(which is 4) and the fourth element (which is 8), then adds them together, resulting in the output 12.

7. Question: Write a C++ code snippet that reads a positive integer n from the user, creates a

vector of size n, fills it with the first n even numbers, and then prints the sum of the vector's elements.

Answer:

1. What is a hash map in C++?

Answer: A hash map, also known as an unordered map in C++, is a container that stores key-value pairs, where each key is associated with a unique value. It allows for fast retrieval, insertion, and deletion of elements based on their keys, as it uses a hash function to map the keys to indices in the underlying data structure.

2. Which header file should be included to use unordered_map in C++?

Answer: To use unordered_map in C++, you need to include the

header file.

3. How do you declare an unordered_map
    with
    int
    as the key and
    string

as the value?

Answer: To declare an

unordered_map

with

int

as the key and

string

as the value, use the following syntax:

4. How do you insert a key-value pair into an
    unordered_map?

Answer: You can insert a key-value pair into an
unordered_map using the

insert()

function or the [] operator. For example:

5. Write a code snippet that counts the frequency
    of words in a vector of strings using an
    unordered_map.

Answer:

6. How do you access the value associated with a
    given key in an unordered_map?

Answer: You can access the value associated with a given key in an unordered_map using the [] operator or the at() function. For example:

7. How do you check if a key exists in an unordered_map?

Answer: You can check if a key exists in an unordered_map using the find() function. If the key is not present in the map, the find() function returns an iterator pointing to the end() of the map. For example:

8. How do you remove an element from an unordered_map given its key?

Answer: You can remove an element from an unordered_map given its key using the erase() function. For example:

Solutions: C++ Sets: The Elite Ensemble of Unique Elements

1. What is a hash set in C++?

Answer: A hash set, also known as an unordered_set in C++, is a container that stores unique elements in no particular order. It allows for fast retrieval, insertion, and deletion of elements, as it uses a hash function to map the elements to indices in the underlying data structure.

2. Which header file should be included to use unordered_set in C++?

Answer: To use unordered_set in C++, you need to include the header file.

3. How do you declare an unordered_set with int as the element type?

Answer: To declare an unordered_set with int as the element type, use the following syntax:

4. How do you insert an element into an unordered_set?

Answer: You can insert an element into an unordered_set using the insert() function. For example:

5. Write a code snippet that removes duplicate elements from a vector of integers using an unordered_set.

Answer:

6. How do you check if an element exists in an unordered_set?

Answer: You can check if an element exists in an unordered_set using the find() function. If the element is not present in the set, the find() function returns an iterator pointing to the end() of the set. For example:

7. How do you remove an element from an unordered_set?

Answer: You can remove an element from an unordered_set using the erase() function. For example:

8. How do you find the number of elements in an unordered_set?

Answer: You can find the number of elements in an

unordered_set

using the

size()

function. For example:

9. Can an unordered_set contain duplicate elements?

Answer: No, an unordered_set cannot contain duplicate elements. Each element in an unordered_set is unique.

10 Write a code snippet that finds the intersection of two unordered_sets of integers.

Answer:

Solutions: C++ Pairs: The Dynamic Duo of Data

1. What is a pair in C++?

Answer: A pair in C++ is a simple container that stores two elements of potentially different types. Pairs are useful when you need to store two related values together as a single entity.

2. Which header file should be included to use pair in C++?

Answer: To use pair in C++, you need to include the

header file.

3. How do you declare a pair with int as the first
   element and string as the second element?

Answer: To declare a pair with int as the

first

element and string as the second element, use the following syntax:

4. How do you assign values to the elements of a pair?

Answer: You can assign values to the elements of a pair using the

first

and second member variables. For example:

5. Write a code snippet that creates a vector of pairs, where each pair contains an integer and its square.

Answer:

6. How can you create a pair using the
    make_pair()
    function?

Answer: You can create a pair using the

make_pair()

function by providing the two values as arguments.
The function will return a pair with the specified
values. For example:

7. How do you access the first and second
    elements of a pair?

Answer: You can access the first and second elements
of a pair using the first and second member variables.
For example:

8. Can a pair be used as a key in an
    unordered_map?

Answer: No, a pair cannot be used as a key in an
unordered_map directly because pairs do not have a
predefined hash function. However, you can use a
pair as a key in a map since map uses a comparison
function instead of a hash function.

9. Write a code snippet that sorts a vector of
    pairs based on the second element in each
    pair.

Answer:

1. What is a struct in C++?

Answer: A struct (short for structure) in C++ is a user-defined data type that groups together variables under a single name. It can store multiple variables of different data types, making it easier to organize and manage related data.

2. How do you define a struct in C++?

Answer: To define a

struct

in C++, use the struct keyword, followed by the name of the struct and its member variables enclosed in curly braces. For example:

3. How do you create an instance of a struct?

Answer: To create an instance of a struct, use the struct's name followed by the instance's name. For example:

4. How do you access the member variables of a struct?

Answer: You can access the member variables of a struct using the dot (.) operator. For example:

5. Write a code snippet that defines a struct Person with the member variables

name

,

age

, and

address

, and creates an instance of the struct.

Answer:

6. Can a struct contain a member function?

Answer: Yes, a struct can contain member functions just like a class. The main difference between structs and classes is the default access specifier: it is

public

for structs and

private

for classes.

7. Can a struct have a constructor?

Answer: Yes, a struct can have a constructor, which is a special member function that initializes the struct's member variables when an instance of the struct is created. For example:

To create an instance of this struct, you can use the following syntax:

8. Can a struct be used as a key in a map or unordered_map?

Answer: Yes, a struct can be used as a key in a map if you provide a custom comparison function. For unordered_map, you need to provide both a custom hash function and an equality operator for the struct.

9. Write a code snippet that sorts a vector of Person
   structs by age.

Answer:

This code defines a

Person

struct and a

compare_by_age

function for comparing two

Person

instances by their age. The

main()

function creates a vector of Person instances and sorts them by age using the

compare_by_age

function. Finally, it prints the sorted list of people.

1. What is a queue data structure in C++? Explain its basic operations.

Answer: A queue is a linear data structure in C++ that follows the First-In-First-Out (FIFO) principle. It allows insertion of elements at the back (enqueue) and removal of elements from the front (dequeue). Basic operations include

push()

,

pop()

,

front()

,

back()

,

empty()

, and

size()

.

2. Which header file is required to use the

queue

container in C++?

Answer: The

header file is required to use the queue container in C++.

3. What is the difference between push() and pop() functions in a queue?

Answer: The

push()

function is used to add an element at the back of the queue, whereas the

pop()

function is used to remove an element from the front of the queue.

4. Write a code snippet that creates a queue of integers, adds the numbers 1 to 5, and then removes and prints the elements until the queue is empty.

5. What will be the output of the following code?

Answer: The output will be 20 30.

6. How can you check if a queue is empty or not?

Answer: You can use the

empty()

function to check if a queue is empty or not. It returns

true

if the queue is empty, otherwise, it returns

false

.

7. Can you use a queue to implement a stack? If yes, explain how.

Answer: Yes, it is possible to implement a stack using two queues. When pushing an element, add it to the non-empty queue. When popping an element, dequeue all but the last element from the non-empty queue and enqueue them into the other queue. Then, dequeue the last element from the non-empty queue. This will be the top of the stack.

8. Write a code snippet to reverse the elements of a queue.
9. What is the time complexity of the
    push()
    and
    pop()
    operations in a queue?

Answer: The time complexity of both

push()

and

pop()

operations in a queue is O(1).

Solutions: C++ Stacks: The Tower of Data Power!

1. What is a stack data structure in C++? Explain its basic operations.

Answer: A stack is a linear data structure in C++ that follows the Last-In-First-Out (LIFO) principle. Basic operations include

push()

(inserting an element at the top),

pop()

(removing the top element),

top()

(accessing the top element),

empty()

(checking if the stack is empty), and

size()

(getting the number of elements).

2. Which header file is required to use the stack container in C++?

Answer: The

header file is required to use the stack container in C++.

3. What is the difference between
   push()
   and
   pop()
   functions in a stack?

Answer: The

push()

function is used to add an element at the top of the stack, whereas the

pop()

function is used to remove the top element from the stack.

4. Write a code snippet that creates a stack of integers, pushes the numbers 1 to 5, and then pops and prints the elements until the stack is empty.
5. What will be the output of the following code?

Answer: The output will be 20.

6.   How can you check if a stack is empty or not?

Answer: You can use the

empty()

function to check if a stack is empty or not. It returns

true

if the stack is empty, otherwise, it returns

false

.

7.   Can you use a stack to implement a queue? If yes, explain how.

Answer: Yes, it is possible to implement a queue using two stacks. When enqueuing an element, push it onto stack 1. When dequeuing an element, if stack 2 is empty, pop all elements from stack 1 and push them onto stack 2, then pop the top element from stack 2. This will be the front of the queue.

8.   Write a code snippet to reverse a string using a stack.

9.   What is the time complexity of the push() and pop() operations in a stack?

Answer: The time complexity of both

push()

and

pop()

operations in a stack is O(1).

10. How can you use a stack to evaluate a postfix expression?

Answer: To evaluate a postfix expression using a stack, iterate through the expression. If the current character is an operand, push it onto the stack. If the current character is an operator, pop the top two operands from the stack, perform the operation, and push the result back onto the stack. When the iteration is complete, the stack

Solutions: The Dynamic Duo - Deque in C++

1. What is a deque in C++ and which header file should be included to use it?

Answer: A deque (double-ended queue) is a dynamic data structure in C++ that allows elements to be added or removed from both the front and the rear. To use deque in your code, you need to include the header file .

2. Write a code snippet to create a deque of integers named intDeque.

3. How do you add elements to the front and back of a deque?

Answer: You can use the member functions

push_front()

and

push_back()

to add elements to the front and back of a deque, respectively.

4. Write a code snippet to add the numbers 1, 2, and 3 to the front of the deque intDeque
.

5. How do you remove elements from the front and back of a deque?

Answer: You can use the member functions pop_front() and pop_back() to remove elements from the front and back of a deque, respectively.

6. Write a code snippet to remove the first and last elements of the deque intDeque
.

7. How do you access the front and back elements of a deque without removing them?

Answer: You can use the member functions

front()

and

back()

to access the front and back elements of a deque without removing them.

8. Write a code snippet that prints the front and back elements of the deque intDeque

.

9. How can you use a deque to implement a stack? Provide an example of pushing an element onto the stack and popping an element from the stack.

Answer: To implement a stack using a deque, you can use the

push_back()

and

pop_back()

functions to push and pop elements, respectively.

10. How can you use a deque to implement a queue? Provide an example of enqueuing an element and dequeuing an element.

Answer: To implement a queue using a deque, you can use the

push_back()

function to enqueue elements and the

pop_front()

function to dequeue elements.

1. What is a graph data structure, and what are its main components?

Answer: A graph is a data structure consisting of a finite set of vertices (or nodes) and a finite set of edges connecting the vertices. The main components of a graph are vertices and edges.

2. What is the difference between a directed and an undirected graph?

Answer: In a directed graph, each edge has an initial vertex (tail) and a terminal vertex (head), indicating a one-way relationship between vertices. In an undirected graph, edges do not have an initial or terminal vertex, indicating a two-way relationship between vertices.

3. Name two common ways to represent a graph in C++.

Answer: Two common ways to represent a graph in C++ are adjacency matrix and adjacency list.

4. Write a code snippet to represent an undirected graph using an adjacency list in C++.

5. What is the time complexity of searching for an edge in an adjacency matrix and an adjacency list?

Answer: The time complexity of searching for an edge in an adjacency matrix is O(1), while in an adjacency list, it is O(V) for an undirected graph and O(E) for a directed graph.

6. What is a weighted graph?

Answer: A weighted graph is a graph in which each edge has an associated weight or cost. The weights can represent distances, costs, capacities, etc.

7. Explain the difference between depth-first search (DFS) and breadth-first search (BFS) algorithms.

Answer: Depth-first search (DFS) is a graph traversal algorithm that explores as far as possible along a branch before backtracking. It can be implemented using recursion or an explicit stack. Breadth-first search (BFS) is a graph traversal algorithm that explores all vertices at the current level before moving on to vertices at the next level. It is implemented using a queue.

8. Write a code snippet to perform a DFS traversal on an undirected graph using recursion.

9.   What are some common graph algorithms?

Answer: Some common graph algorithms are depth-first search (DFS), breadth-first search (BFS), Dijkstra's shortest path algorithm, Bellman-Ford algorithm, Kruskal's minimum spanning tree algorithm, Prim's minimum spanning tree algorithm, and Floyd-Warshall algorithm.

10.   Explain how you would detect a cycle in an undirected graph using DFS.

Answer: To detect a cycle in an undirected graph using DFS, start a DFS traversal from every unvisited node. During the traversal, if you encounter a node that has been visited and is not the parent of the current node, then there is a cycle in the graph.

Solutions: A Tale of Two Complexities: Runtime and Space in the Algorithmic Kingdom

1.   What is time complexity in the context of algorithms?

Answer: Time complexity is the amount of time an algorithm takes to run as a function of the size of the input data. It provides an estimation of the performance of an algorithm, helping to compare different algorithms and determine which one is more efficient for a specific task.

2.   What is space complexity in the context of algorithms?

Answer: Space complexity is the amount of memory an algorithm uses as a function of the size of the input data. It provides an estimation of the memory requirements of an algorithm, helping to compare different algorithms and determine which one is more memory-efficient for a specific task.

3.   What is the Big O notation, and what does it represent?

Answer: Big O notation is a way to describe the performance of an algorithm by representing the upper bound of its growth rate. It shows the relationship between the size of the input data and the number of operations or memory usage, allowing for a comparison of different algorithms' efficiency.

4.   What is the time complexity of the following code snippet?

Answer: The time complexity of this code snippet is O(n^2) because there are two nested loops, each running for 'n' iterations.

5.   What is the space complexity of the following code snippet?

Answer: The space complexity of this code snippet is O(1) because the memory usage does not depend on the size of the input array. Only a single integer variable 'sum' is used, which occupies constant space.

6.   What is the time complexity of the binary search algorithm?

Answer: The time complexity of the binary search algorithm is O(log n) because, in each iteration, the search space is reduced by half.

7. Write a code snippet for a function that has a time complexity of O(n) and space complexity of O(n).

8. How does the time complexity of the Quick Sort algorithm change in the worst-case, average-case, and best-case scenarios?

Answer: For the Quick Sort algorithm, the time complexity is O(n^2) in the worst-case scenario, O(n log n) in the average-case scenario, and O(n log n) in the best-case scenario.

9. What is the time complexity of the Merge Sort algorithm, and what is its space complexity?

Answer: The time complexity of the Merge Sort algorithm is O(n log n) in all scenarios (worst-case, average-case, and best-case). Its space complexity is O(n), as it requires additional memory for the merging process.

10. Explain the difference between constant time (O(1)), linear time (O(n)), and quadratic time (O(n^2)) complexities.

- Constant time (O(1)) complexity refers to an algorithm whose execution time remains constant regardless of the input size. Examples include array access, basic arithmetic operations, and simple statements.

- Linear time ($O(n)$) complexity refers to an algorithm whose execution time is directly proportional to the input size. As the input size increases, the time taken by the algorithm increases linearly. Examples include simple loops, searching for an element in an array, or summing the elements of an array.
- Quadratic time ($O(n^2)$) complexity refers to an algorithm whose execution time is proportional to the square of the input size. As the input size increases, the time taken by the algorithm increases quadratically. Examples include nested loops, bubble sort, and insertion sort.

In summary, constant time complexity represents algorithms with constant execution time, regardless of input size; linear time complexity represents algorithms whose execution time is proportional to the input size; and quadratic time complexity represents algorithms whose execution time is proportional to the square of the input size.

Solutions: The Fabulous Four: Marvelous Min, Mighty Max, Astounding Avg, and Sensational Sum in C++

1. Write a C++ function that takes an array of integers and returns the maximum value in the array.
2. What is the output of the following code snippet?

Answer: The output will be

, as the code calculates the sum of the elements in the

numbers

array.

3. Write a C++ function that calculates the average of the elements in a vector of doubles.

Answer:

4. Given a vector of integers, write a C++ function that returns a pair containing the minimum and maximum values in the vector.
5. What is the time complexity of finding the minimum value in an array of integers?

Answer: The time complexity is O(n), where n is the number of elements in the array.

6. Write a C++ function that takes an array of integers and its size, then returns the index of the maximum value in the array.
7. Write a C++ function that calculates the sum of all even numbers in a given vector of integers.
8. What is the output of the following code snippet?

Answer: The output will be

120

, as the code calculates the product of the elements in the

numbers

vector.

9. Write a C++ function that calculates the average of all odd numbers in a given vector of integers.

1. Name the two most commonly used sorting algorithms in C++'s Standard Library.

    Answer: The two most commonly used sorting algorithms in C++'s Standard Library are std::sort()
    and
    std::stable_sort()
    .

2. Write a C++ code snippet that sorts a vector of integers in ascending order using std::sort()
    .

3. What is the time complexity of the std::sort()
    function?

Answer: The time complexity of std::sort() is O(n log n), where n is the number of elements being sorted.

4. Write a C++ function that sorts a vector of strings in descending order using std::sort()

   .

5. How do you sort a vector of custom objects based on a specific attribute using std::sort()
   ?

You can use a custom comparison function or a lambda function as the third argument of std::sort(). This function should take two objects as arguments and return a boolean value that represents the desired sorting order. For example:

6. Question: What is the main difference between std::sort()
   and
   std::stable_sort()
   ?

Answer: The main difference is that

std::stable_sort()

maintains the relative order of elements with equal values, while

std::sort()

does not guarantee this.

7. Question: Write a C++ code snippet that sorts an array of integers in descending order using std::sort()

.

8. How can you sort a
   std::list
   of integers in ascending order?

Answer: You can use the member function std::list::sort() to sort the list in ascending order. For example:

9. How do you use
   std::partial_sort()
   to find the k smallest elements in a vector of integers?

Answer: You can use std::partial_sort() to sort the first k elements in the vector. For example:

10. How can you use `std::sort()` to sort a vector of integers based on their absolute values?

Answer: You can use a custom comparison function or a lambda function as the third argument of `std::sort()`. This function should take two integers as arguments and return a boolean value that represents the desired sorting order based on their absolute values. For example:

std::lower_bound()

function?

Answer: The time complexity of

std::lower_bound()

is O(log n), where n is the size of the vector. It uses binary search to find the first occurrence of the given element or the position where the element would be inserted to maintain the sorted order.

6. Write a code snippet that finds the first occurrence of the value 42 in a sorted std::vector called numbers using std::lower_bound()

    .

7. What is the time complexity of searching for an element in an unordered_set ?

The average time complexity of searching for an element in an

std::unordered_set

is O(1). However, in the worst case, it can be O(n), where n is the size of the unordered_set.

8. Can you use binary search on a linked list? Why or why not?

No. Binary search requires random access to elements in a collection, which means you can access any element in constant time. However, a linked list does not provide constant-time random access to elements because each element is only accessible by traversing the list starting from the head node.

As a result, binary search cannot be directly applied to a singly-linked list in its standard form.

To use binary search on a linked list, you would need to modify the standard binary search algorithm to work with a linked list by keeping track of the mid-point of the list and traversing the list accordingly. This would require finding the length of the list, which would take linear time, and then performing binary search by traversing the list in O(log n) time.

Therefore, while it is possible to use binary search on a linked list, it would not be efficient as compared to other data structures such as an array or a balanced binary search tree.

Solutions: The Adventures of Simulation & Brute Force: Tales of Complete Search in C++

1. What is a brute force (complete search) algorithm?

Answer: A brute force (complete search) algorithm is an approach where all possible solutions to a problem are generated and checked to find the correct solution. This method is usually simple to implement but can be inefficient, especially for large input sizes.

2. What is the time complexity of a brute force algorithm that checks all combinations of N elements?

Answer: The time complexity of a brute force algorithm that checks all combinations of N elements is usually O(2^N) since it explores all possible subsets of the input set. However, the complexity may vary depending on the specific problem and implementation.

3. Write a function that finds the maximum sum subarray of a given vector using a brute force approach.

4. Describe a situation where using a brute force algorithm would be appropriate.

Answer: A brute force algorithm is appropriate when the input size is small, the problem's solution space is not too large, or when you need a quick and easy-to-implement solution to verify the correctness of a more efficient algorithm.

5. Write a function that checks if a given string is a palindrome using a brute force approach.

6. Write a brute force algorithm to find the greatest common divisor (GCD) of two integers.

7. Given a list of integers, find all the subsets that have a sum equal to a target value using a brute force approach.

8. Write a brute force algorithm to find the longest common subsequence (LCS) of two strings.
9. Using a brute force approach, find the number of ways to make change for a given amount using a set of coin denominations.
10. What are the main disadvantages of using brute force algorithms?

Answer: The main disadvantages of brute force algorithms are their inefficiency and poor performance, especially for large input sizes. Brute force algorithms often have high time and/or space complexity, which makes them impractical for solving real-world problems with large inputs. However, they can be useful for small inputs or when used to verify the correctness of a more efficient algorithm.

Solutions: Greedy Algorithms: The Swift, the Smart, and the Validated

1. What is a greedy algorithm?

Answer: A greedy algorithm is a problem-solving approach that makes the locally optimal choice at each step with the hope of finding a globally optimal solution. It focuses on making the best possible decision at each stage, without considering the overall problem or future consequences.

2. Mention a popular problem where a greedy algorithm provides an optimal solution.

Answer: The popular problem where a greedy algorithm provides an optimal solution is the "Fractional Knapsack Problem". In this problem, we have a knapsack with a given capacity and a set of items with different weights and values. The objective is to maximize the total value of the items in the knapsack, and we are allowed to take fractions of the items.

3. Explain the greedy algorithm for the fractional knapsack problem.

Answer: The greedy algorithm for the fractional knapsack problem is as follows:

- Calculate the value per unit weight (value/weight) for each item.
- Sort the items in descending order based on their value per unit weight.
- Select items from the sorted list until the knapsack is full, taking as much of each item as possible.

4. Write a C++ function to implement the greedy algorithm for the fractional knapsack problem.

5. Can greedy algorithms always guarantee an optimal solution?

Answer: No, greedy algorithms cannot always guarantee an optimal solution. They work well for certain problems, like the fractional knapsack problem, but may produce suboptimal solutions for other problems, such as the 0/1 knapsack problem or the traveling salesman problem.

6. Explain the greedy algorithm for the coin change problem.

Answer: The greedy algorithm for the coin change problem is as follows:

- Sort the coin denominations in descending order.
- Start with the largest denomination and use as many coins as possible without exceeding the target amount.
- Move to the next largest denomination and repeat the process until the target amount is reached or there are no more denominations left.

7. Does the greedy algorithm for the coin change problem always produce the minimum number of coins required?

Answer: No, the greedy algorithm for the coin change problem does not always produce the minimum number of coins required. It works well for certain sets of coin denominations, like the U.S. coin system, but may produce suboptimal solutions for other sets of denominations.

8. What are some advantages of using greedy algorithms?

Answer: Some advantages of using greedy algorithms are their simplicity, ease of implementation, and relatively lower time complexity compared to other algorithms. They can often provide a good approximate solution to a problem, even if it is not guaranteed to be optimal.

9. Implement a greedy algorithm to find the minimum number of intervals needed to cover a given set of intervals.

10. Explain the activity selection problem and how a greedy algorithm can be used to solve it.

Answer: The activity selection problem involves choosing the maximum number of non-overlapping activities that can be performed, given a set of activities with start and end times. A greedy algorithm can be used to solve this problem by selecting activities based on their earliest finishing times. The algorithm sorts the activities by their end times and iterativel

Solutions: Recursion: Unraveling the Magical Loops of Code

1. What is recursion in C++?

Answer: Recursion is a programming technique where a function calls itself in order to solve a smaller version of the same problem. This process continues until a base case is reached, which is the simplest version of the problem that can be solved directly.

2. Write a recursive function to calculate the factorial of a non-negative integer

n

.

3. Write a recursive function to compute the nth Fibonacci number.
4. Explain the difference between direct and indirect recursion.

Answer: Direct recursion occurs when a function calls itself directly within its body, while indirect recursion occurs when a function calls another function, which in turn calls the first function.

5. How can you avoid stack overflow in a recursive function?

Answer: To avoid stack overflow in a recursive function, you can use techniques such as memoization to store intermediate results, or rewrite the function using an iterative approach instead of recursion.

6. Write a recursive function to find the greatest common divisor (GCD) of two integers using the Euclidean algorithm.
7. Write a recursive function to calculate the sum of an array of integers.
8. Write a recursive function to reverse a string.
9. Explain tail recursion and how it is different from regular recursion.

Answer: Tail recursion is a special case of recursion where the recursive call is the last operation in the function. In tail recursion, the compiler can optimize the function by reusing the existing stack frame, eliminating the need for additional stack frames. This can lead to improved performance and reduced memory usage compared to regular recursion.

10. Write a recursive function to find the height of a binary tree.